Musterion
A Biblical Primer on Prophecy

William H. Noah

William H Noah
I Cor 13

Avalon
P R E S S

www.avalonpress.net

Scripture references are from
the 1769 Cambridge Edition King James Bible

ISBN
0-9724708-1-6 Price $12.00

To Melody,
Mary Lu, Margaret, Meredith,
my mother, Ruth
and in memory of my dad, Terry Sr.

Other titles offered by author
William H. Noah and Avalon Press

The First Commandment
Be Fruitful, and Multiply

The First Commandment II
Sun, Water, and Soil
(coming Fall of 2003)

**From the Dead Sea Scrolls
to the Forbidden Book**
The Origins of the English Bible

TABLE OF CONTENTS

FOREWORD

Many Christians are beginning to experience a fresh hunger for God. Not just for His blessings and provision, but for Him. We want to encounter His person and hear His voice. Yet the pursuit of these desires seems a bit too mystical, particularly when we question whether we personally could receive a revelation or prophecy from God. We seek guidance from other believers, but to whom should we listen? One friend suggests these things no longer exist and cautions against "charismatic" indulgences. Another of equal sincerity affirms our openness to the movement of the Spirit, ready to introduce us to a world of uninterpreted tongues, unconfirmed prophecies, and euphoric spiritual pandemonium. Confronted with these paths, we fear our future will be characterized either by lifeless dogma, directionless sailing, or even worse —abandonment of the quest.

If you identify with these struggles, do not despair. There is hope! With sound exegesis of the original languages of the Scripture, *Musterion: A Biblical Primer on Prophecy* explores the process of God revealing His mysteries and His treasures to those who seek Him. It examines the biblical meaning of prophecy, its role in the Old and New Testaments, and its purpose for the body of Christ today. Christian, it has been ordained for you. If you are a true seeker of God, it is likely that you have already received spiritual mysteries and shared them with others. Indeed, the insights shared herein are a paradigm of revelation and this book, a paradigm of prophecy.

Musterion: A Biblical Primer on Prophecy does not answer all the questions. It may best be described as a primer for greater intimacy with God. Test each word of this book against the Scripture, and if it be confirmed, do not harden your heart. Instead, humble yourself, listen for His still, small voice, and prepare to be changed as you encounter His Word. May it all be for the glory of Christ Jesus.

John Kea, J.D.

INTRODUCTION

The word "prophecy" in the Bible is translated from the Greek word *prophetes*, which stems from *pro*, meaning "beforehand," and *phemi*, meaning "to tell." Thus, to prophesy is to speak beforehand or to foretell, and a prophet would be a foreteller of the future, or one who speaks beforehand. This understanding of prophecy as future-telling or a prophet as a mere teller of the future is common in many churches today but may be too limited. Although the apostle Paul wrote that prophecy should be a key element in a church meeting (1 Cor. 14:29–31), prophecy, by this definition, is most uncommon in today's assemblies.

Some define prophecy to mean "speaking for God"; thus, when someone is preaching or teaching from the Bible, he is speaking for God and thus prophesying. Using this definition, we see that prophecy is quite prevalent in today's meetings, but is this understanding accurate? In contrast, there are others who believe that prophecy, while clearly evident in Old Testament times and in the early church, mostly disappeared after the New Testament writings were compiled because the Bible replaced the role of the prophet. What is the correct definition of prophecy? Does it still exist in the church today? If so, how does it manifest itself? These questions puzzled me for years, but then something happened.

Because of an emergency at the hospital, I was late to my friend Gary's house for Bible study one night. A local pastor was visiting and causing quite a stir with his viewpoint that the Bible must be understood in the context of church history. He said that any teaching or prophecy (if it still exists) must be compared to the writings of historical church leaders and the summaries of the great church councils to ensure their consistency with established doctrine. New teachings or revelations differing from the majority view of the church must be rejected. He believed that it was the function of the organized church to preserve "pure" doctrine or truth, and that the role of the prophet had been mostly replaced. If a prophet did arise, then the mainstream church doctrine could be used to judge whether he was a true or false prophet.

He said that throughout church history, anyone who strayed from this "pure" doctrine would have been branded a heretic and that even questioning such teaching could be dangerous to us spiritually. Furthermore, he added that this was how cults develop: someone would experience a revelation from Scripture and teach what he thought was truth without verifying this new truth with mainstream church teaching.

Yes, this process of only accepting homogenous thoughts would prevent differing viewpoints that could lead to factions or cults. But which majority view do we, all of us Christians, accept? To which denominational doctrine do we conform? How do we even know that these church councils or influential church leaders were correct? After all, the Apostles' Creed is not in the Bible, and Paul did not write the Westminster Confession.

I knew that revelation or prophecy must be tested against the Scriptures and not church doctrine, but I was unsure of the process and could not begin to explain it. Therefore, I spent the next week wondering if I was a heretic myself, on the verge of starting a new cult. Then I sat again on Gary's couch the next week in ignorance as the discussion on prophecy proceeded around me. If the discussion did lead to a consensus opinion on prophecy, it might just be another council decree. Instead of the Council of Nicaea or the Council of Chalcedon, this would be the Council of Gary's Living Room. Like the previous church councils throughout history, our decree might still be the opinion of man and not God. I needed a revelation on revelation.

My Bible was open, so I just started to read from 1 Corinthians 13. And as I started to turn the page, I saw an answer! It was right in front of me. I had read the passage a hundred times yet never saw it before. It was not that I understood the answer immediately, but I found the definition of prophecy in 1 Corinthians 13:2. It was a cool drink of spring water to a soul that had thirsted many years for this answer.

Jesus implied that we are all spiritually blinded (John 9:39) and must wait on the Spirit of God to open our eyes to truth. This insight usually occurs line by line, precept upon precept (Isa. 28:10). We do not actually teach truth; we merely reveal what has been revealed to us by God's Spirit. We must then be diligent, like the Bereans (Acts 17:11), and search the Scriptures to verify the revelation, and not being so concerned with other tangential writings.

I will never forget sitting on that couch. Just as the Lord spoke to Jacob at El-Bethel (Gen. 35:7), He still speaks to

His children today, for I heard the Lord in Gary's living room. In these pages, we will examine this manifestation called prophecy and comprehend that the revelations from God's Spirit are the "true riches" (Luke 16:11) of His kingdom. Jesus Christ still reveals Himself to man today, and from these revelations, men and women still prophesy. Please understand that I, like Paul, only "know in part, and … prophesy in part" (1 Cor. 13:9). In other words, I have not seen the complete picture, but what I have seen, Lord willing, I share with you, the reader.

Chapter 1
Prophecy Defined:
The Mysteries of God

As I was sitting on Gary's couch that evening, I read
1 Corinthians 13:1–3:

> Though I speak with the tongues of men and of
> angels, and have not charity [love], I am become
> as sounding brass, or a tinkling cymbal. *And*
> *though I have the gift of prophecy, and understand*
> *all mysteries, and all knowledge*; and though I have
> all faith, so that I could remove mountains, and
> have not charity [love], I am nothing. And
> though I bestow all my goods to feed the poor,
> and though I give my body to be burned, and
> have not charity [love], it profiteth me nothing.
> (emphasis added)

In these verses, Paul used hyperbole, or exaggeration, to emphasize the point of teaching: the primacy of love. Hyperbole was a rhetorical practice of Paul throughout his letters, and probably the most recognizable example is Romans 6:1–2: "What shall we say then? Shall we continue in sin, that grace may abound? God forbid. How shall we, that are dead to sin, live any longer therein?" Paul used hyperbole to emphasize the ridiculous thought of sinning repeatedly merely to experience grace, and he utilized the same rhetorical device here in 1 Corinthians 13.

Paul addressed five different manifestations of the Spirit in 1 Corinthians 13:1–3: tongues, prophecy, faith, giving, and service. He exaggerated the extent of language or tongues to include that of angels. He exaggerated the manifestation of prophecy to the point where it allows understanding of *all* mysteries and *all* knowledge of God. He exaggerated faith to the point where faith removes mountains, and he exaggerated giving to the point where giving demands all of one's possessions. Finally, he exaggerated service to where service requires giving one's body to be burned.

Now, *exaggeration* may be an imprecise word to use since there are Christians in times past and present who have demonstrated such acts of giving and service. *Epitome* may be a better word. The epitome of giving is sacrificing all of one's possessions to feed the poor. The epitome of faith is being able to remove mountains, and the epitome of prophecy is to know *all* mysteries and *all* knowledge of God.

If the ultimate accomplishment in prophecy is to know and understand all mysteries and all knowledge of God, then prophecy may be simply defined as knowing the mysteries and knowledge of God. Even though Paul used poetic hyperbole for emphasis, what he said is still true. The spiritual manifestation or gift of prophecy proclaims knowledge of the mysteries and knowledge of God. Within this teaching on the superiority of love through Paul's hyperbole, God has hidden the definition of prophecy. This is what the Lord revealed to me that Wednesday night. But what are the mysteries and knowledge of God?

Musterion

The Greek word for "mystery" used throughout the New Testament is *musterion*, simply meaning "secret" or "hidden." In English, the word *mystery* comes from this Greek word *musterion*, but we have imbued the word with an element of intrigue. In the Greek, this sense of intrigue may not be intended. *Musterion* in Scripture denotes a spiritual truth that is hidden or concealed within an allegory or parable. For instance, Mark 4:10–11 says, "And when he [Jesus] was alone, they that were about him with the twelve [disciples] asked of him the parable. And he said unto them, *Unto you it is given to know the mystery of the kingdom of God: but unto them that are without* [outside], *all these things are done in parables*" (emphasis added). In other words, only those who

3

were in a close (intimate) relationship with Jesus were given the interpretation, while the multitude (not close to Him) only heard the parable. The spiritual truth, or mystery, is hidden within the parable, and Jesus simply revealed the meaning of the parable to those in a close relationship with Him. In the same way today, Jesus reveals the hidden secrets or mysteries concerning His kingdom to those who are in an intimate relationship with Him. Receiving this private, secret knowledge of Him, as denoted by the Greek word *musterion*, is part and parcel of prophecy. When children of the kingdom of God share secret truths about the kingdom and its King (Jesus), they are prophesying.

Musterion comes from the Greek word *mueo*, meaning "to be taught a secret." *Mueo* occurs only once in the New Testament, in Philippians 4:12 where it is translated, "I am *instructed* [*mueo*] both to be full and to be hungry, both to abound and to suffer need" (emphasis added). The word "mystery" or "mysteries" occurs in the New Testament twenty-seven times and refers to approximately ten to twenty different mysteries or secrets within the kingdom of God. For instance, there is the "mystery of His will" (Eph. 1:9) and the "mystery of Christ" (Eph. 3:4; Col. 4:3). There is a "great mystery" (Eph. 5:32) concerning Christ and His bride. There is the "mystery of faith" (1 Tim. 3:9) and the "mystery of godliness" (1 Tim. 3:16). There is the "mystery of iniquity" (2 Thess. 2:7) and the "mystery of the woman" called Babylon (Rev. 17:5, 7). There is the "mystery of God" (Col. 2:2) that Revelation 10:7 says "should be finished" during the time of the seventh (last) angel sounding his trumpet. Thus, at that time, the secrets of God will be finished and all will be revealed.

In 1 Corinthians 15:51–52, Paul said, "Behold, *I shew you a mystery* [secret]; We shall not all sleep, but we shall all be changed, In a moment, in the twinkling of an eye, *at the last trump*: for the trumpet shall sound, and the dead shall be raised incorruptible, and we shall be changed" (emphasis added). Here the apostle Paul referred to a secret or mystery at the time of the last, or seventh, trumpet: "The dead shall be raised incorruptible, and we [who remain] shall be changed." At the time of this seventh trumpet, the mystery or secret of God will be finished: "*But in the days of the voice of the seventh angel, when he shall begin to sound [his trumpet], the mystery of God should be finished, as he hath declared to his servants the prophets*" (Rev. 10:7, emphasis added). At this last trumpet, the secret of God is finished, suggesting there are no more secrets or mysteries, and thus no more prophecy. Here also we see that God has revealed His mystery, or secret, to His prophets. If God reveals this mystery to His prophets, and His prophets interpret or proclaim the secret to others, then prophets are those who reveal or explain the secrets of God. Once again, prophecy can be defined as revealing the secrets or hidden truths of God.

Revealed by the Spirit

Only the Spirit of God can reveal His mysteries, and this process of prophecy is a manifestation of the Holy Spirit. Look at 1 Corinthians 2:6–13:

Howbeit we speak wisdom among them that are perfect: yet not the wisdom of this world, nor of the princes of this world, that come to nought: *But we speak the wisdom of God in a mystery* [secret], *even the hidden wisdom, which God ordained before the world* unto our glory: Which none of the princes of this world knew: for had they known it, they would not have crucified the Lord of glory. But as it is written, Eye hath not seen, nor ear heard, neither have entered into the heart of man, the things which God hath prepared for them that love him. *But God hath revealed them unto us by his Spirit: for the Spirit searches all things, yea, the deep things of God.* For what man knoweth the things of a man, save the spirit of man which is in him? even so the things of God knoweth no man, but the Spirit of God. Now we have received, not the spirit of the world, but the spirit which is of God; *that we might know the things that are freely given to us of God. Which things also we speak, not in the words which*

*man's wisdom teacheth, but which the Holy Ghost
teacheth; comparing spiritual things with spiritual.*
(emphasis added)

Those of us who are married to Christ (in an intimate relationship with Him) will speak God's wisdom as in a mystery
or secret. The speaking or revealing of this mystery or secret
is prophecy. Verse 7 goes on to mention "the hidden wisdom,
which God ordained before the world unto our glory," meaning that the wisdom of God is hidden, or secret, and God
determined this before the world began.

No effort of man's flesh can see God's secrets. No searching from one end of the earth to the other by our souls can
find any secret of God. Verse 9 says that this hidden wisdom
was prepared beforehand, only for those "that love him." The
princes of this world do not know God's wisdom, neither
have their eyes seen nor their ears heard the secret things of
God: "But God hath revealed them [mysteries] unto us [His
children] by his Spirit: for the Spirit searcheth all things, yea,
the deep things of God" (v. 10). Only the Spirit Himself can
search for the wisdom of God and find the deep, hidden
secrets of God contained in the Scripture and His creation.

We must not only be born of the Spirit (John 3:5) in
order to search for the mysteries of God, but we must walk in
His Spirit (Rom. 8:14) in order to find the truths of God.
Searching is not so much a condition of the mind as it is a
condition of the heart. Once our hearts have been made right

7

with God, then our minds can be renewed (Rom. 12:1–2), and we can "have the mind of Christ" (1 Cor. 2:16).

Just as each person has private thoughts within his mind that others do not know, no man knows the thoughts of God. Only the Spirit of God knows the thoughts of God. Look at 1 Corinthians 2:11–12: "*For what man knoweth the things of a man, save the spirit of man which is in him? even so the things of God knoweth no man, but the Spirit of God.* Now we have received, not the spirit of the world, but the spirit which is of God; that we might know the things that are freely given to us of God" (emphasis added). As a husband would reveal his private thoughts and secrets only to a wife who is faithful and intimate, God reveals His thoughts and secrets only to those who are faithful and intimate with Him. Those of us who have received "the spirit which is of God" are to know the secret things "that are freely given to us of God."

First Corinthians 2:13 tells us that the Holy Spirit is to personally teach us this hidden wisdom. We do not have to learn from man; the Holy Spirit is the real teacher. A purpose of the new covenant (New Testament) is that we can be taught of God directly by His Spirit. "And ye need not that any man teach you: but as the same anointing teacheth you of all things, and is truth, and is no lie, and even as it hath taught you, ye shall abide in him" (1 John 2:27). We no longer need Moses or any man to teach us as prophesied in the Old Testament: "And they shall teach no more every man his neighbour, and every man his brother, saying, know the

LORD: for they shall all know me, from the least of them unto the greatest of them, saith the LORD" (Jer. 31:34). Sure, we can hear God through an intermediary (other than Jesus) such as a friend, but it is not God's first choice. God can speak to us through any means, even a donkey (Num. 22:28), but He desires us to hear Him directly (John 10:27).

Jesus is our only Mediator (1 Tim. 2:5) and our High Priest (Heb. 7:24–28). Those of us who know the Lord are also priests (Rev. 5:10) but to a lost, dying world and not to each other. We are brothers and sisters. When we choose to look to an intermediary or priest today, we fall back to the ways of the old covenant. It is often a blessing to receive teaching from others, but we do not have to be taught by others: "Now we have received, not the spirit of the world, but the Spirit which is of God; *that we might know the things that are freely given to us of God"* (1 Cor. 2:12, emphasis added).

Revelation and Prophecy

A closer examination of the word *revealed* will demonstrate the relationship between revelation and prophecy. The Greek word for revealed, in 1 Corinthians 2:10, is *apokalupto*. It comes from the Greek words *apo*, meaning "from," and *kalupto*, meaning "to conceal or cover." *Kalupto* implies "a covering, such as skin, bark, a shell, or veil." *Apokalupto* is a verb, meaning "to remove the cover, veil, or skin," bringing into open view that which was hidden. Its noun is *apokalupsis* and means "revelation," such as the "Revelation to John the Apostle." Again, *apokalupsis* is an uncovering, a disclosure, an unveiling, a manifestation, or a revelation.

Now, when something is concealed or covered from open view, it is hidden. It lies in secret under a veil, a skin, or a covering. First Corinthians 2:10 refers to a revealing or uncovering of "hidden" wisdom by the Spirit of God. Therefore, revelation uncovers, unveils, and reveals the hidden wisdom or mysteries of God. This is the definition the Scripture gives for prophecy. To have a revelation from the Spirit of God is to receive truth, knowledge, or secret wisdom from God by having it unveiled. The act of revealing is prophesying; thus, one who reveals the secrets or mysteries of God is a prophet.

Revelation leads to prophecy. First Corinthians 14:29–30 says, "Let the prophets speak two or three, and let the other judge. If any thing be *revealed to another that sitteth by*, let the first hold his peace" (emphasis added). In this passage, Paul is giving specific instructions on how the body of Christ is to assemble. He cast these instructions in stone in verse 37 by saying, "*The things I write unto you are the commandments of the Lord*" (emphasis added). Because he commanded that two or three prophets should speak and verse 31 suggests that all present may prophesy, it appears that two or three may involve a minimum number.

Nevertheless, if another sitting in the meeting receives a revelation, the one speaking is to be silent (v. 30).

Therefore, picture these prophets uncovering the mysteries or secrets of God to the body, and suddenly another sitting by is given hidden wisdom or a revealed mystery and begins to share. What the one sitting is sharing is called a revelation in verse 30 but is referred to as prophecy in verse 31. Therefore, we see again the association or, more precisely, the interchangeable use of prophecy and revelation. In fact, prophecy is revelation by the Spirit of God. False prophecy or false teaching would be revelation from the father of all lies, the devil (John 8:44).

Before we proceed further, we should understand that some might describe these manifestations as "gifts" of the Spirit because the Scripture specifically says "the gift of prophecy" in 1 Corinthians 13:2. However, the word *gift* does not occur in the Greek in this verse or in other verses where so-called "gifts of the Spirit" are mentioned. For instance, in the previous chapter where the text says, "Now concerning spiritual gifts" (1 Cor. 12:1), the Greek simply reads *pneumatikos*, meaning "concerning spirituals." The Greek words *dorea* and *doron*, meaning "gift," do not occur in this verse, and a more accurate translation might be "Now concerning spiritual matters." Prophecy, therefore, may not be a "gift" for just the select Christian but a blessing for all the children of God.

In conclusion, prophecy is knowing the secrets or mysteries of God. It is receiving the hidden wisdom or knowledge of the kingdom of God. It is a manifestation of the Holy Spirit and is often misrepresented as a "gift" in English translations.

Though the wisdom or secret is given to us, we are not given the ability to prophesy. Only the Spirit of God has this ability, and our souls are merely given the revelation or knowledge. We must "walk" in His Spirit to prophesy and see "the deep and secret things" of God (Dan. 2:22). As we will later see, these deep things are covered and must be uncovered, or revealed. The revelation of the hidden things of God is prophecy.

Chapter 2
Prophecy Defined
in the Old Testament

As we continue this study, let us look for the definition of
prophecy within the Old Testament. Amos 3:7 says, *"But he
[God] revealeth his secret unto his servants the prophets"* (emphasis added). Clearly this verse is consistent with the definition
of prophecy that we uncovered in the New Testament.
Specifically, this verse is quite similar to Revelation 10:7,
which states that God declares His mystery, or secret, to His
servants the prophets. Here again in Amos, God is revealing
(uncovering) His mysteries unto His servants the prophets.
Because a prophet is one who prophesies, then prophecy must
again be meant as the revealing of the secrets of God.

The Hebrew word translated as "secret" in this verse is
transliterated as *cowd* and pronounced as "sode." It is translated "secret" but has an aspect of intimacy associated with
it. One might say "an intimate secret" is a more accurate ren-

dering from the Hebrew. *Cowd* may also be considered private knowledge. In Proverbs 11:13 and 20:19, we are warned about sharing our "private" secrets, or *cowd*, with a "talebearer," otherwise known as a gossip. Sharing these intimate secrets, private knowledge, and private information without the permission of the person violates his trust. In fact, one only shares such information with one he can trust. And only an unwise person shares such information with a gossip. I can assure you that God is wise.

During the time of Job, this concept of God's secret already existed. Even Job's friends knew something about the concept because in Job 15:8, Eliphaz the Temanite asked Job, "Hast thou *heard the secret [cowd] of God*? and dost thou restrain wisdom to thyself?" (emphasis added) Later, in chapter 29, Job continued his parable and spoke of a previous day when he was more intimate with God and said, "As I was in the days of my youth, when the secret *[cowd]* of God was upon my tabernacle [temporary shelter]" (v. 4, emphasis added). In both these verses, the Hebrew word *cowd* indicates intimate knowledge through a close relationship.

Just as we read in the New Testament, the secrets of God are shared only with those who are intimate with Him and faithful. Since fear is the "beginning of knowledge" (Prov. 1:7) and "the beginning of wisdom" (Prov. 9:10), God's secrets are revealed only to those who fear Him: "*The secret of the LORD is with them that fear him*; and he will shew them his covenant"(Ps. 25:14, emphasis added). The secret of the Lord is only for those in relationship or covenant with Him. It is only for the righteous: "For the froward [stubborn] is abomination to the LORD: *but his secret is with the righteous"* (Prov. 3:32, emphasis added). In these verses from Psalms and Proverbs, the word "secret" is also the Hebrew word *cowd.*

The Prophet Daniel

In 586 B.C., the kingdom of Judah was finally taken into captivity by the kingdom of Babylon under King Nebuchadnezzar. Daniel was probably a small boy when the captivity began, and he was trained in all the ways of the Chaldeans (Babylonians). Because of his faithfulness, through the providence of God, he was promoted to the second-highest position in the kingdom. He reported only to King Nebuchadnezzar. Because of his intimate relationship with God, as well as his faithfulness, God revealed to him many secrets that are recorded in the book of Daniel.

During these seventy years of captivity, some of Daniel's Hebrew language was replaced with the Chaldean equivalent. The word "secret" in the book of Daniel is mainly from the word *raz*, pronounced "rawz." It is of Chaldean origin and means "something hidden, a secret or a mystery." For example, Daniel 2:17–23 says:

> Then Daniel went to his house, and made the thing known to Hananiah, Mishael, and Azariah [Shadrach, Meshach, Abednego], his companions:

That they would desire mercies of the God of heaven concerning this secret [raz]; that Daniel and his fellows should not perish with the rest of the wise men of Babylon. *Then was the secret [raz] revealed unto Daniel in a night vision.* Then Daniel blessed the God of heaven. Daniel answered and said, Blessed be the name of God for ever and ever: for wisdom and might are his. And he changeth the times and the seasons: he removeth kings, and setteth up kings: *he giveth wisdom unto the wise, and knowledge to them that know understanding: He revealeth the deep and secret things: he knoweth what is in the darkness, and the light dwelleth with him.* I thank thee, and praise thee, O thou God of my fathers, who hast given me wisdom and might, and hast made known unto me now what we desired of thee: for thou hast now made known unto us the king's matter. (emphasis added)

It was Daniel's greatest desire—for his own life and the lives of his friends depended on it—to know the secret and interpret the dream of the king. Daniel said that the God of heaven revealed the secret unto him (in a night vision). He acknowledged that the wisdom he received actually came from God. God revealed to Daniel a mystery in that He revealed both King Nebuchadnezzar's dream and its interpretation.

And after the revelation is given, "The king answered unto Daniel, and said, Of a truth it is, that your God is a God of gods, and a Lord of kings, *and a revealer of secrets, seeing thou couldest reveal this secret*" (Dan. 2:47, emphasis added). Because Daniel made it clear that the mystery revealed was by God, God received all honor and praise. King Nebuchadnezzar actually offered a definition of prophecy himself in verse 47, when he said that Daniel's God was "*a revealer of secrets*" (emphasis added). And as God reveals these secrets, His prophets speak the revelation and, thus, prophesy. The prophet Daniel revealed the secrets of God to Nebuchadnezzar, thus again defining prophecy for us as revealing the mysteries or secrets of God.

The Deep Things of God

If we look again at Daniel 2:22, Daniel proclaimed (referring to God), "He revealeth the deep and secret things: he knoweth what is in the darkness, and the light dwelleth with him." The word for "secret" in this verse is *cethar*, pronounced "sethar," meaning "to conceal" and is again Chaldean in origin. This verse contains additional aspects pertaining to the concepts of revelation and prophecy that we have yet to discuss. Notice the reference to "deep and secret things." The word "deep" is *amiyq* and of Chaldean origin, meaning "profound, deep, or unsearchable." It is derived from another Chaldean word representing depth, and thus, it refers to things under the surface. Since the Greek word *apokalupto* means "uncovering or unveiling," then the secret or hidden things are deep and under the surface, a shell, the skin, or possibly the bark of a tree. They are secret and hidden by the covering; thus removing the covering brings them to the surface and reveals the secret.

Yet, the deep or profound things of God are further under the surface. In other words, they have a greater amount of covering and, thus, need a greater amount of revelation or unveiling. This greater uncovering or debarking requires great patience and persistence in seeking God. Just as it takes time in a relationship to get to the deepest issues, it takes years in relationship with God for Him to reveal His deepest mysteries.

Searching the deep things of God might be described as jumping into a bottomless pit called the knowledge of God. As we fall farther into this hole and the Spirit uncovers deeper levels to reveal deeper truth, we begin to see more and more of the Lord Jesus. Yes, we see through a mirror dimly now (1 Cor. 13:12), and the image is still distorted. But the more time we spend seeking our Husband, the Lord Jesus, the more glimpses we get of Him. We must wait upon the "incorruptible" to come upon us at the last trumpet when we will see Him "face to face" (v. 12). Then, all the veils and coverings will be removed, and all the secrets will be revealed. Then there will be no distortion in our view of Him, and we will no longer be shallow in our understanding of Him: "That Christ may dwell in your hearts by faith; that ye, being rooted and grounded in love, *May be able to comprehend with all saints what is the breadth, and length, and depth, and height; And to know the love of Christ, which passeth knowledge,* that ye might be filled with all the fulness of God" (Eph. 3:17–19, emphasis added).

The Light of Revelation

As we look further at Daniel 2:22, we see another aspect of revelation from God: "He [God] knoweth what is in the darkness, and the light dwelleth with him." Things that lie in darkness are hidden from our eyes. Things that lie in darkness are in secret. They are a mystery, and, of course, God knows all mysteries and all knowledge since they are all of Him. Therefore, He knows whatever lies in darkness. Secondly, "the light dwelleth with Him" as the apostle John said, "God is light, and in him is no darkness at all" (1 John 1:5). Now when things lie in darkness and are hidden, they can be revealed only one way—by light. And since the light dwells with God, only God (through the Holy Spirit) can reveal what is in the darkness. While it is in darkness, it is secret, but once the light shines upon it, the darkness evaporates, and what once lurked in mystery is now visible before our eyes and, thus, revealed. Just as we have seen so far, prophecy is revealing the secret or hidden things of God, and it is pictured as light shining through the darkness.

Genesis 1:3–4 says, "And God said, Let there be light: and there was light. And God saw the light, that it was good: and God divided the light from the darkness." He declared the light as good, and on that first day of creation, He started doing something that He continues to do constantly until the mystery of God will be complete at the last trumpet: He separates light from darkness. He said that light can have no fellowship with darkness (1 John 1:6–7), and furthermore, darkness cannot overtake the light, but the light merely ceases to shine: "Ye are all children of light, and the children of the day: we are not of the night, nor of darkness. Therefore let us not sleep, as do others; but let us watch and be sober"(1 Thess. 5:5–6). The closer we stand to the lamp, the Lamb of God (Rev. 21:23), the more light we receive. In the same way, the closer we are in relationship to Lord Jesus, the more revelation we will receive. The closer we are to the Lord Jesus, the more He will reveal His mysteries to us.

Conceptualized as light shining in the darkness, revelation by the Spirit of God is a great blessing. We should seek a deeper relationship and, thus, deeper understanding of the Lord. We should repent of our shallow relationships with Him which are fostered by our lack of interest in spending time with God and by mentalities too easily focused on merely being entertained. Instead of peppering our speech with "catchy," religious, "feel good" phrases, so common at church meetings, we should seek to speak the deep, secret things of God. We should speak like Daniel and Amos did. We should, as Paul revealed, seek to prophesy and reveal the mysteries of God (1 Cor. 14:5,12,19).

Chapter 3
Prophecy and Tongues

The definition of prophecy is also further demonstrated in the comparison of prophecy to tongues. In the beginning of chapter 14 of 1 Corinthians, Paul wrote:

> Follow after charity [love], and desire spiritual gifts [manifestations], but rather [more so] that ye may prophesy. For he that speaketh in an unknown tongue speaketh not unto men, but unto God: for no man understandeth him; *howbeit in the spirit he speaketh mysteries. But he that prophesieth speaketh unto men to edification, and exhortation, and comfort. He that speaketh in an unknown tongue edifieth himself; but he that prophesieth edifieth the church. I would that ye all spake with tongues, but rather that ye prophesied: for greater is he that prophesieth than he that*

speaketh with tongues, except he interpret, that the church may receive edifying. Now brethren, if I come unto you speaking with tongues, what shall I profit you, except I shall speak to you either by revelation, or by knowledge, or by prophesying, or by doctrine [teaching]? And even things without life giving sound, whether pipe or harp, except they give a distinction in the sounds, how shall it be known what is piped or harped? For if the trumpet give an uncertain sound, who shall prepare himself to the battle? *So likewise ye, except ye utter by the tongue words easy to be understood, how shall it be known what is spoken?* for ye shall speak into the air. There are, it may be, so many kinds of voices in the world, and none of them is without signification. Therefore if I know not the meaning of the voice, I shall be unto him that speaketh a barbarian, and he that speaketh shall be a barbarian unto me. *Even so ye, forasmuch as ye are zealous of spiritual gifts, seek that ye that may excel to the edifying of the church. Wherefore let him that speaketh in an unknown tongue pray that he may interpret.* For if I pray in an unknown tongue, my spirit prayeth, but my understanding is unfruitful. What is it then? I will pray with the spirit, and I will pray with understanding also: I will sing with the spirit, and I will sing with the understanding also. Else when thou shalt bless with the spirit, how shall he that occupieth the room of the unlearned say Amen at thy giving of thanks, seeing he understandeth not what thou sayeth? For thou verily givest thanks well, but the other is not edified. I thank my God, I speak with tongues more than ye all: *Yet in the church I had rather speak five words with my understanding, that by my voice I might teach others also, than ten thousand words in an unknown tongue.* (vv. 1–19, emphasis added)

In this tremendous passage, Paul repeatedly demonstrated the superiority of prophecy over tongues. In the kingdom of God, the focus is on others and not ourselves. The true child of God shows concern for his brother's burdens (Gal. 6:2) and loves his neighbor as himself (Rom. 13:9). Therefore, that which edifies others is superior to that which edifies only self. Prophecy, which edifies the body of Christ, is greater than tongues, which edifies only self (unless interpreted).

Even though prophecy is superior, speaking in tongues does exist. This passage plainly tells us that tongues can exist as an individual's experience under the influence of the Holy Spirit (v. 2). Paul clearly expressed that speaking in tongues does have value (v. 4) and is a great blessing to the one speaking. The child of God praying or singing in this unknown tongue is edified (v. 4) but has no understanding or revelation

(v. 14). Paul said he desired to pray and sing in the Spirit but with understanding (v. 15). He went on to say he would rather utter "five words with my understanding" than "ten thousand words in an unknown tongue" (v. 19).

Although there is value in speaking only "unto God" in tongues, there is much greater value in prophesying, which benefits the whole body of Christ. However, if the unknown tongue is interpreted so that the church may hear and understand, receiving edification, then tongues is equal to prophecy. In fact, Paul wanted all believers to speak in tongues (v. 5) because the tongue is such an instrument of edification to the speaker and, when interpreted, to the church. An "uninterpreted" tongue has no value for the body and, therefore, has much less importance than prophecy.

The child of God who speaks in an unknown tongue is speaking the mysteries or secrets of God: "For he that speaketh in an unknown tongue ... in the spirit he speaketh mysteries" (v. 2). If the ability to interpret this mystery equates the tongue with prophecy, then again, we see the definition of prophecy as interpreting or revealing the mysteries of God.

As we saw in 1 Corinthians 13, love is greater than giving, serving, prophesying, and speaking in tongues, and love is the first of the "fruit of the Spirit" listed in Galatians 5:22–23. First Corinthians 14:14 says that praying in an unknown tongue makes our understanding "unfruitful." The Greek word for "unfruitful" is *akarpos*, meaning "without fruit." Praying in unknown tongues does not produce fruit of the

Spirit, such as love. It may be a great blessing to those who possess this manifestation of the Spirit, but without understanding or interpretation, it does not produce love, joy, peace, patience, gentleness, goodness, faith, meekness, and self-control (Gal. 5:22–23). Paul wished that we all experience this manifestation of tongues, but more so that we prophesy, and even more that we produce fruit, such as love.

Revelation, Knowledge, Prophecy, and Teaching

Uninterpreted tongues may not be useful to the body, but revelation, knowledge, prophecy, and teaching are of great profit to the body of Christ: "Now, brethren, if I come unto you speaking with tongues, what shall I profit you, *except I shall speak to you either by revelation, or by knowledge, or by prophesying, or by doctrine* [teaching]?" (1 Cor. 14:6, emphasis added). Earlier we defined revelation as the uncovering or unveiling of something hidden or secret, as in this case, the mysteries of God. Knowledge is information, and in this verse is signified by the Greek word *gnosis*, which is from the Greek word *ginosko*. It means intimate knowledge gained through experience in a relationship. The knowledge referred to here in verse 6 is not casual information concerning God but intimate knowledge He would reveal only to a faithful "friend" like Abraham, or His bride.

Up to this point, we have used prophecy and revelation almost interchangeably, and in most circumstances, this is fine. However, more specifically, revelation is the knowledge we receive through the Spirit, and prophecy is when we share the revelation with others. Revelation is given to an individual while prophecy is given to the body (church). Prophecy requires knowing the mysteries and knowledge of God through revelations by His Spirit.

Teaching involves relating to the body, the church, what God has revealed to us through His Spirit and how the Scriptures verify the revelations we received. Anytime we receive revelation, we should study the Scriptures with a right heart toward God to see if the thought came from our souls or from the Spirit (Heb. 4:12). As Paul wrote in his second letter to the church at Corinth, we must bring "into captivity every thought to the obedience of Christ" (10:5). As we examine our revelations in accordance with Scripture, we provide a basis of knowledge for teaching. We also are able to question or even reject those "revelations" not consistent with Scripture. We may conclude that these false or incomplete revelations originated from some other source and not from God's Spirit.

This is why the Bereans were more "noble" than the Thessalonians (Acts 17:11). These Bereans were open to any new revelation or teaching, but they searched the Scriptures daily to verify the teaching for themselves. Those who read this work should likewise seek the Lord privately to see if this is, in fact, truth.

Division over Experience

As a personal note, I have never spoken knowingly in an unknown tongue. In addition, I have never been in a meeting where an unknown tongue was subsequently interpreted, and where I was then edified. Only a foolish person would claim expertise at something he has never experienced, and I have never personally experienced tongues. Yet I know from Scripture that tongues occur and may be common. I have asked the Lord, as well as fellow brothers who speak in tongues, why I have never manifested this evidence of the Spirit. After all, I thank God for the existence of tongues today in the body of Christ and furthermore am convinced that it should be quite common, as Paul desired that we all speak in tongues. I have close brothers who have spoken and do speak in unknown tongues. Interestingly, the ones with this manifestation in which I see the fruit of the Spirit (love, joy, peace, patience, goodness, kindness, humility, faith, and self-control) never draw attention to themselves with the tongue and never speak an uninterpreted tongue in assembly.

I have a strong desire to see unity in the body of Christ, and, unfortunately, this issue of tongues is a major dividing factor today. I know that Christ is not coming back for a harem but for a single bride, who shall be one, as He and the Father are one (John 17:21). If I speak in tongues, my endorsement of tongues might be viewed as an endorsement of my own experience. Because I do not personally possess this manifestation, those who do not speak in tongues may be able to consider my case. Paul taught that tongues existed in his day in the body of Christ for the purpose of edifying the individual believer (1 Cor. 14:4). Unless the Holy Spirit has changed or the Scripture no longer applies, then we must acknowledge the existence of tongues for personal edification and their equality with prophecy, if correctly interpreted. We must thank God for this evidence of His Spirit, even if we do not possess it ourselves. I am like Paul in that I wish that all Christians (including myself) spoke in tongues. It is merely Paul's wish and mine; it is not God's, or else all believers would speak in tongues.

Unfortunately, there are some individuals who teach that the evidence of the Holy Spirit in a Christian's life is the presence of tongues. This is not true. Jesus never says, "Ye shall know them by their tongues." He says, "Wherefore by their fruits ye shall know them" (Matt. 7:20). We will know the brethren only by the fruit of the Spirit: love, joy, peace, patience, kindness, goodness, faithfulness, gentleness, and self-control. Fruit is superior to tongues and prophecy.

Without the presence of the fruit of love, a person who speaks in tongues is merely a loud, irrelevant noise. Paul said, "Though I speak with tongues of men and of angels, and have not charity [love], I am become as sounding brass, or a tinkling cymbal"(1 Cor. 13:1). In the same way, without love, prophecy and knowledge mean absolutely nothing. In Matthew 7:15–23, Jesus said that there would be those who prophesy, cast out demons, and do "wonderful works" in His name but never even know (*ginosko*) Him. The Lord warns us not to be deceived by great works or signs but to look for fruit. Fruit is the evidence of God's Spirit. When we look at others' lives for light, we should look for fruit and not signs.

When we look at our own lives, we should examine whether we hear His voice. Jesus never says, "My sheep speak in tongues or prophesy." He says, "My sheep hear my voice" (John 10:27). Jesus never says, "He that is of God speaketh in tongues or prophesieth." He says, "He that is of God heareth God's words: ye therefore hear them not, because ye are not of God" (John 8:47).

We must seek to hear His voice and seek to bear the fruit of the Spirit. Just as the seeds that multiply the apple trees are inside the apple, the seeds that multiply the kingdom of God are inside the fruit of the Spirit: "For if I pray in an unknown tongue, my spirit prayeth, but my understanding is *unfruitful*" (1 Cor. 14:14, emphasis added). Again, speaking in an unknown tongue does not produce fruit and, thus, cannot have seed; it will not multiply the kingdom of God. Though tongues are a great blessing to many, we must seek to be fruitful in our understanding.

A problem with tongues arises from indoctrinating or making law out of our own experience. This may stem from insecurity, leading to pride and causing division. As examples, we should examine both extreme views involving tongues. First is the Christian who does not manifest tongues and may feel insecure about not having this manifestation. He may think to himself that God loves him as much as all His other children, and if God were going to give this manifestation to any of His children, He would certainly give it to him. Therefore, he decides if he does not speak in tongues, they must not exist, and all these "so-called" Christians running around speaking in tongues are deceived in their understanding.

It may be from this extreme view that the teaching came forth that tongues existed only in the time of the early church before A.D. 300, and since we now have the Bible, there is no further need for this manifestation. First Corinthians 13:10 is commonly used to imply that the Bible is the "perfect" to come, suggesting that tongues, prophecy, and knowledge all ceased at this time. (In chapter 5, I will more fully discuss why this is not so.) One must be careful when proposing that a New Testament manifestation of God's Spirit after Pentecost no longer exists. Certainly, we would have to have ample Scripture to make such a point. So far in my study of the Scriptures, I simply have not found any Scripture to support the idea that tongues have ceased.

At the other extreme, we have a similar problem in the body of Christ today, concerning those who speak in tongues. Brothers and sisters who speak in tongues can begin to base the security of their relationship with God on the presence of their tongues; whereas Scripture teaches we should base the security of our relationship with Jesus on hearing His voice and manifesting the fruit of the Spirit. Because a believer enjoys the manifestation of tongues, he might begin to focus on this outward occurrence, instead of the inner condition of the heart. He may think all believers should speak in tongues and twist verses out of context to endorse his experience. The desire of Paul that all Christians would speak in tongues is exaggerated into a law that all Christians should or even must speak in tongues. Unfortunately, some even teach that the main evidence for the Spirit in a believer's life is speaking in tongues and not fruit. When Jesus returns at the end of the age for the great harvest, He will be looking for fruit, not tongues (Matt. 7:20). A harvest is always for fruit. Again, we must not make law out of our own experience (or the lack thereof).

Whether one sides on one extreme or the other, the result is a divided body. Each side judges the other's relationship with Christ based on the presence or absence of tongues, instead of on the fruit of the Spirit. We cannot all have the same experiences, and in spite of this, we must be one as Jesus and the Father are one (John 17:21). This same problem occurred in the Corinthian church, and Paul admonished them,

> *Brethren, be not children in understanding: how be it in malice be ye children, but in understanding be men.* In the law it is written, With men of other tongues and other lips will I speak unto this people; and yet for all that will they not hear me, saith the Lord. Wherefore tongues are

for a sign, not to them that believe, but to them
that believe not: the prophesying serveth not for
them that believe not, but for them which
believe. (1 Cor. 14:20–22, emphasis added)

The Corinthians were also immature in their understanding
of tongues, and this was causing strife and malice in their day
just as it does today.

Unfortunately, we are all somewhat bound by our own
experiences, and we tend to congregate mostly with those
who have had (or not had) similar experiences so that our
souls feel safe and comfortable. This is not the will of God:
God desires us to be uncomfortable so that we will not trust
in the men around us, but in Him alone. Jesus said, "And ye
shall know the truth, and the truth shall make you free"
(John 8:32). Only the truth can set us free from the bondage
of our experience and the need to be accepted by man. But
we can know the truth only through understanding, and
understanding must come as a revelation of the Spirit. This
again is prophecy, and is equated with an interpreted tongue.

Chapter 4
Prophesy in Part

Prophecy never gives complete knowledge. As I previously said, I only have a partial understanding because God has revealed only part of the secret concerning prophecy to me. Paul admits he prophesied only in part and knew in part (1 Cor. 13:9), and even though he said, "Be ye followers [imitators] of me, even as I also am of Christ" (1 Cor. 11:1), he had only partial understanding. Paul's part may have been larger than most others, but it was still just part of the picture. We must be humble and careful what we boast in. This is especially true for understanding and doctrine.

Paul said,

> *Charity* [love] *never faileth*: but whether there be prophecies, they shall fail; whether there be tongues, they shall cease; whether there be knowledge, it shall vanish away. *For we know in part,*

and we prophesy in part. But when that which is
perfect is come, then that which is in part shall be
done away. When I was a child, I spake as a child,
I understood as a child, I thought as a child: but
when I became a man, I put away childish things.
For now we see through a glass, darkly; but then
face to face: now I know in part; but then shall I
know even as also I am known. (1 Cor. 13:8–12,
emphasis added)

Paul continued to demonstrate the superiority of the fruit of
the Spirit, such as charity (love), over manifestations of the
Spirit, such as prophecy, tongues, or knowledge. This is why
the first commandment recorded in the Bible is "Be fruitful
and multiply" (Gen. 1:28). We are to bear love and the other
fruit, because fruit will never fail; it will endure forever in the
kingdom of God, on the tree of life (Rev. 22:2).

While the fruit of the Spirit is eternal, verse 8 clearly says
that prophecies, tongues and knowledge will, at some time
in the future, vanish. It is interesting that the Greek word
signifying the termination of prophecy and knowledge in
verse 8 is the same—*katargeo.* This word implies a cessation
or ending that is accomplished by force and is permanent. It
is not a temporary or partial cessation. In other words, at
some time after the writing of this letter by Paul, prophecy
and revealed knowledge of the kingdom of God will be terminated permanently.

In a similar fashion, at some point in the future, tongues will cease as well. The Greek word used for their termination is *pauo*, which is where we get our English word *pause*. Although very similar to *katargeo*, it is not as strong and can be a temporary cessation. To place this in the twenty-first-century vernacular, consider a video recorder. *Pauo* would be the pause button, whereas *katargeo* would be the stop button.

We saw earlier that prophecy is revealing the mysteries of the kingdom of God, which leads to knowledge. Thus, prophecy or revelation precedes knowledge, as knowledge is the result of prophecy or revelation. The linkage between these two is evident again in that the same Greek word (*katargeo*) is used for their termination. At this time in the future, when prophecy is abolished, knowledge will be abolished as well since there is no more prophecy to produce knowledge. Tongues will also cease at some point, but because of the use of a different Greek word, there is suggestion that this cessation will not be permanent.

The prophet Daniel also spoke of a time when prophecy and vision would end. Daniel 9:24 says, "Seventy weeks are determined upon thy people and upon thy holy city, to finish the transgression, and to make an end of sins, and to make reconciliation for iniquity, and to bring in everlasting righteousness, and to seal up the vision and prophecy, and to anoint the most Holy." Sometime during or more likely at the end of these seventy weeks of years (490 years), vision and prophecy will be "sealed up." The Hebrew word for "sealed" is *chathan* and means "to end, close, seal, or stop." In fact, in the same verse, this word *chathan* is also translated "to make an end" regarding sins. So it appears that Daniel, like Paul, was referring to a time in the future when prophecy will end or stop, and this time of closure will occur at the end of Daniel's prophecy.

Until this future time when cessation occurs, we are to continue to prophesy, have knowledge, and speak in tongues as the Lord wills, but we are to remember that we know only "in part, and we prophesy in part" (1 Cor. 13:9). This experiential knowledge, signified by the Greek word *ginosko*, refers to only partial knowledge. Revelation of the secrets of God, defined as prophecy, is only partial as well. The word translated "part" in 1 Corinthians 13:9 is the Greek word *merismos*, a noun signifying "that which is divided or shared." In other words, we have only part or a share of the knowledge of God. One may say that knowledge and prophecy give only a partial share of the understanding of God and should tend to keep us humble, remembering that the Bible says, "Who hath known the mind of the Lord? or who hath been his counselor?" (Rom. 11:34)

When we are ready to complain or argue a situation or circumstance, we should remember that we have only partial knowledge or a share of the information. Therefore, we should always yield the decision to the one who has all the information: God. We should abide by the will of Him who has all knowledge and who is an unbiased and loving leader.

This is why we should abide by the will of the Father. We have a Father in heaven who has complete knowledge, complete understanding, and complete interest in us, yet we often do not desire His decisions or His will because we do not trust: "Without faith it is impossible to please him" (Heb. 11:6).

Explore New Land

A picture of this partial understanding of prophecy is contained in the word *merismos*. A derivative of this Greek word *merismos* is *meros*, meaning "a coastline" (Matt. 15:21, 16:13; Acts 19:1). To understand this partial understanding that prophecy gives, we should consider the explorers of a previous time viewing new land from a ship. When they looked toward the land, they could see only part; they could not tell if it was a small island or a major continent because they could see only the coastline. So it is with understanding the depths of God: we can see only the small part that is revealed. But as we land "our ships" on the coastline and go deeper and deeper into the territory, more and more is revealed.

Just think: As we study and the Holy Spirit begins to reveal things to us, we are like the explorer of a new continent. As we walk each day by faith, God reveals "new land" to us. As for the explorers of the New World, our initial revelation pertains to just the coastline or a mere part of the whole. We must explore further and further to find new revelations.

But even after surveying the general landscape, an explorer could spend an eternity examining a small part. In fact, just from the atomic level and larger, one square inch of land would yield information to study for a million lifetimes; so it is with the knowledge of God.

The prophet Daniel had a revelation of the kingdom of God as a great mountain (Dan. 2), and he may have thought that it was very near him in proximity. In actuality, the mountain was far away. The arrival of the kingdom of God (the great mountain) was fulfilled spiritually with the first advent of Christ (more than five hundred years after Daniel) when God's will was done in heaven. The physical fulfillment of God's will being "done in earth, as it is in heaven" (Matt. 6:10) will be when "the kingdoms of this world are become the kingdoms of our Lord, and of his Christ; and he shall reign for ever and ever" (Rev. 11:15). This is the mountain that Daniel saw. To Daniel, this great mountain may have appeared on the coastline, but it was far, far inland. We must always be careful when we receive revelation, especially concerning future events. Prophecy is partial, and we often are not given a specific time frame.

This partial understanding ought to encourage unity in the body of Christ. We should realize that our revelations are incomplete and be careful not to add to them out of our own understanding. But as humans under the curse, our pride often leads us to try to answer everyone's questions completely, instead of just offering only the part that the Holy

Spirit revealed to us. Furthermore, those listening to us are cursed as well and want complete understanding themselves, so true teachers and prophets are often rejected because their understanding or revelation is just in part while people want complete answers to their questions.

As we fill in the "gaps" of our knowledge purely out of our own understanding, we produce factions and divisions within the body of Christ. This is because everyone has his own understanding or follows the understanding of others. If we could all simply follow one Spirit and be content in the partial answer we are given, we would have unity. The addition may come from our minds but all lies originate with the father of lies, who is Satan (John 8:44). It is our additions to Scripture that cause contradicting viewpoints, and trusting in these differences leads to factions and divisions in the body of Christ: "Trust in the LORD with all thine heart; and lean not unto thine own understanding" (Prov. 3:5). *We must not be lovers of doctrine or understanding but lovers of truth.*

Search for Gold

We must learn to extract the small amount of truth present in the teachings of men. We must separate truth as the miner separates the gold and silver from the rock. Truth is valuable because it is so rare; we each have so little. Picking and digging, we eventually find one little nugget. And it is worth all the work to find one little "something" that is so valuable. After receiving revelation from God, we must search the Scriptures like the Bereans before we can accept the nugget as truth. This scriptural verification is the refining fire (Rev. 3:18).

Remember, truth tends to be found inside as gold is found in veins inside the rock. As we dig and dig in the Scriptures, we find a small piece of truth. Unfortunately, our pride tends to think that is all there is. At the same time, another brother is digging in another place and finds another nugget of truth. Again, his pride may cause him to think that is all there is as well. This certainty will lead to factions. Instead of arguing and dividing from our brother, we should be open to one another's revelations and study together to find the connection. As veins of gold run through the rock at different levels, so does God's truth. As we chip away and uncover different levels through revelation, we must realize we alone do not have a complete picture of the lengths and breadths and depths of the valuable material that still lies hidden within.

We should consider veins of truth as Michelangelo visualized sculpture. The story is commonly told that when asked how he produced such a beautiful sculpture from a piece of marble, Michaelangelo said he saw the sculpture inside the rock and that he simply had to chip away the part that was not sculpture. In other words, he exposed or revealed the sculpture as he removed that which was not part of the sculpture.

We are like sculptors with works in progress. We may not be able to give others a complete picture of the truth on any subject, but we can continue to chip away at what is not truth. Through the Spirit, we continue to expose fallen man's understanding within us, as well as within our culture. In addition, we must expose this within the church. Just as Michelangelo chipped away that which was not beautiful to find the beauty within the rock, we continue to chip away at false teaching, poor translation, and tradition to find the vein of truth hidden within.

Furthermore, just as the miner can be deceived with fool's gold, we can be deceived with false truth. As we dig away to find the truth of God, Satan is constantly providing us with lies (John 8:44). Just as it takes someone with wisdom and experience to determine fool's gold from the real thing, it takes someone with wisdom in the Scriptures to determine truth from lies. The lies are plentiful; they sound logical; they are loud and confident. A lie looks good, pleases the flesh, and produces pride.

Truth produces humility and always causes a change in our thinking and our practice. We can never receive truth without it changing our thoughts, our understanding, and our life. Lies will often allow us to continue to be separated from God, but truth draws us closer to God. Like the surgeon's knife or the needle of a syringe, initially the truth hurts, but it brings healing later. Truth is like an x-ray for a patient: it produces panic when the cancer is seen, but once the cancer is treated, we rejoice in and are thankful for the x-ray that reveals our problem. Truth is such a blessing; it is so valuable. We must love the truth and hate the lie. You cannot love Jesus without loving the truth—the two can't be separated. Jesus said, "*I am* the way, *the truth*, and the life: no man cometh unto the Father, but by me" (John 14:6, emphasis added).

Chapter 5
The "Perfect" to Come

We have learned that at some time in the future, this partial or limited knowledge produced by prophecy will be forcibly and permanently abolished. First Corinthians 13:10 says, "But when that which is perfect is come, *then that which is in part shall be done away*" (emphasis added). In the future, the partial, represented by the Greek word *meros,* "shall be done away." The Greek word translated "shall be done away" is again *katargeo,* meaning a forcible, permanent termination. The "partial" in this verse represents prophecy and knowledge.

The "partial" prophecy and knowledge will be terminated "when that which is perfect is come" (1 Cor. 13:10). At some time in the future, this "perfect" will arrive or appear, causing prophecy and knowledge to be permanently terminated. I would think that this perfect that comes in the future would be what Daniel referred to (Dan. 9:24) that would put an end to prophecy as well.

Later in the first letter to the Corinthians, Paul wrote, "For now we see through a glass, darkly; but then face to face: now I know in part but then shall I know even as also I am known" (13:12). The second half of this verse says, "Now I *know* in part; but then shall I *know* even as also I am known" (emphasis added). Paul said that he had partial knowledge through experience, represented by the Greek word *ginosko*, and we have learned that his knowledge resulted from prophecy (which is also partial). At some time in the future, Paul would know fully as he was fully known, suggesting he would have complete or full understanding just as "something else" had complete or full understanding of him at the time he was writing. God is the only one who had complete and full understanding of Paul, and at some time in the future Paul would mutually have a full understanding of Him. We currently are like Paul and have only the partial knowledge or partial revelation of Christ, but at some time in the future we will have complete knowledge, and the partial will be abolished. The time when this partial will be done away with and the full knowledge will arrive is again "when that which is perfect is come" (v. 10).

Is the Bible the "Perfect"?

I have heard some say that the "perfect" that was to come (relative to Paul's writing this letter in the first century) is the Bible. Specifically, it has been taught that the "perfect" that was to come was the compilation of the complete New Testament in the third or fourth century A.D. (The oldest complete manuscripts known today date to the fourth century.) Some teach that this occurred in the first century A.D. when the last book of the New Testament was written. Now this "perfect" would have been in the future relative to Paul but is some 1,600 years in our past. If the compilation of the first Greek New Testament is the "perfect" which was to come to Paul, then at the time it was compiled, prophecy and knowledge should have been abolished, and tongues should have ceased as well. They did not, but, unfortunately, this is widely taught today by many.

Many teach that these manifestations of prophecy, knowledge, and tongues (referred to as gifts) ended in the third century or before the time when the New Testament was compiled. Some would believe that the prophet has been replaced by the local preacher or Sunday school teacher, and the apostle has been replaced by the seminary professor. If this compiled Greek New Testament is truly the "perfect" that was to come, then truly prophecy, knowledge, and tongues should have ended at the same time.

The Bible is not the "perfect" that was to come for several reasons pointed out in 1 Corinthians 13:10–12. First of all, the end of verse 12 suggests that at the time the "perfect" arrives or appears "then shall I know even as also I am known." When the "perfect" arrives, I will completely know just as I am completely known by God, and the partial knowledge will be destroyed. The partial knowledge in verse 12 is from the Greek word *ginosko*, which we know is intimate knowledge through experience. This complete or full knowledge by which God knows us is translated from *epiginosko*. The prefix *epi* means "over or full" and, thus, denotes a full or complete knowledge. When this "perfect" arrives, we are to know (*epiginosko*) as well as God knows (*epiginosko*) us.

The longer we are in a relationship with God and the more we learn, the more obvious it becomes what we do not know. One clear observation here is that God understands and knows us in a way far beyond how we could ever know Him in this current, corruptible state. Currently, we cannot even fathom *epiginosko*, so, again, the "perfect" has not come. The Bible does not even give complete understanding or knowledge of God. Jesus told the Pharisees in John 5:39, "[Ye] search the scriptures; for in them ye think ye have eternal life: and they are they which testify of me." The Bible merely points to Jesus. The more I read the Bible, the less I think I know, but the more I see Jesus. This reading aided by the Spirit gives only a partial revealing of Him.

In fact, the word *perfect* is a poor word to describe the Bible. Our translations are far from perfect and are occasionally even distorted by the understanding and bias of the translators. Many today say the Bible is inerrant—meaning completely free from error—but which version, which edition, and which manuscript? As an example, some believe the King James Version (KJV) of 1611 to be inerrant. The KJV

47

may be a more literal, and possibly a more accurate translation than many modern versions in English, but it certainly is not perfect. The KJV we buy today is not even the 1611 version; it is usually a 1769 or later edition. In fact, the 1611 had fourteen additional books that are not in a KJV today.

Although the New Testament was most likely written in Greek, the oldest fragments we have are from a translation into Syriac called the Peshitto. The letters that Paul wrote under the inspiration of the Holy Spirit may have been inerrant, but we do not have them today. Before the discovery of the Dead Sea scrolls in 1948, the oldest Hebrew text (Old Testament) we had was from the ninth century A.D., while Moses had compiled the first five books more than two thousand years earlier. What Moses wrote may have been perfect, but the Bible I hold today merely reveals the Perfect, who is Jesus.

When the New Testament books were compiled in the third century, they were not even perfect. The oldest three Greek manuscripts we have today are not the original writings of Paul, John, Peter, and others. In fact, there are minute variations among these manuscripts. The variations do not affect the message, but they are still not perfect or inerrant. And yet, though our translations are not inerrant, all Scripture is inspired by God. (For a fuller discussion of this topic, see the book *From the Dead Sea Scrolls to the Forbidden Book,* Avalon Press, 2003.)

Perhaps the reason we do not have any of the original copies is precisely because they are perfect. Maybe God wants to be sure we do not confuse His intended "perfect" and the original papers that the New Testament letters and Gospels were written upon. The "perfect" is not the Bible; only Jesus is "perfect."

We should look at the first half of 1 Corinthians 13:12: "For now we see through a glass, darkly; but then face to face." At this point Paul described how he looked through a glass (often translated "a mirror") darkly or in obscurity, but at some point in the future, he would see this "perfect" face-to-face. The word for "mirror" or "glass" in this passage is *eisopsomai*, meaning "to look into." (The same word is used in James 1:23 and obviously is a mirror.) The word *glass* was used to describe a mirror in the seventeenth century by the King James Bible translators, but Paul certainly had no glass in mind when he wrote this letter because mirrors at the time of Jesus were made of polished metals and did not have overlaid glass as we have today. Images were often hazy and usually distorted. Paul said our vision through this mirror is darkly, or obscure. It is interesting that the Greek word *ainigma*, meaning "obscure" or "a hint," is where we get our English word *enigma*. As we look at this mirror, we see an enigma, a puzzle, a riddle, or an obscure or partial image. We see only part of the image until the "perfect" comes, and, thus, we have only partial understanding.

The word "perfect" from 1 Corinthians 13:10 is translated from the Greek word *teleios*, meaning "complete, mature, or of full age." Verse 10 could read: "But when that which is [complete] is come, then that which is in part shall be done away." Obviously, when completion of something occurs, the partial or incomplete is gone. Prophecy, which is partial, will disappear when the complete arrives. Partial knowledge (*ginosko*) will be replaced with "complete" knowledge (*epiginosko*). The partial image through an ancient mirror will be a complete image when the "perfect" arrives.

We have only partial understanding of a distorted and often hazy image, but when that which is perfect is come, then we will see "face to face." There will be no more veil to remove; there will be no more layers or coverings to remove; there will be no more distortion or haziness; there will be no more riddles, puzzles, or enigmas that need prophecy and revelation to expose the true meaning; and there will be no more need for knowledge. At that time, we will see fully, and we will know fully, as we are fully known by the Lord. The "complete" or "perfect" will have arrived, and the partial will be abolished.

The "Perfect" Is Jesus

That appointed time is when the Lord Jesus returns for the marriage supper of the Lamb, after His bride has made herself ready (Rev. 19). As the groom and the bride turn face-to-face at the end of a wedding today, so shall we meet the Lord Jesus face-to-face, for He is the "perfect" that is to come: "Be ye therefore perfect, even as your Father which is in heaven is perfect" (Matt. 5:48).

We will not meet the Bible face-to-face, but we will meet the Lord Jesus face-to-face. There will be no more need for prophecy or knowledge, for the partial (mirror) will be discarded. In addition, tongues will cease temporarily, and we will know fully as we are fully known. Daniel said it will take until the time for the "perfect" to come "to finish the transgression, and to make an end of sins, and to make reconciliation for iniquity, and to bring an everlasting righteousness, and *to seal up the vision and prophecy*, and to anoint the most Holy [Jesus]" (Dan. 9:24, emphasis added).

Finally, Paul wrote in 1 Corinthians 13:11, "When I was a child, I spake as a child, I understood as a child, I thought as a child: but when I became a man, I put away childish things." The Greek word for "child" in this verse is *nepios* and is often translated "infant." It is actually a conjunction of two words: *ne*, meaning "not," and *epos*, meaning "word." It means literally "not word" or one who cannot speak and hence the frequent translation as "child" or "infant." Paul was saying that when he was unable to speak (a child), he spoke as one unable to speak (a child); he understood as one not able to speak, and he thought as one not able to speak (a child); but when he became a man he put these limitations away. This verse may very well be implying the cessation of tongues at the time the perfection occurs. Speaking in tongues would be the language of an infant who speaks, yet there are no recognizable words. The infant speaks a mystery without understanding.

When Paul came to full maturity as a physical man, he put away the childish or infantlike aspects that made him unable to speak. In the same way, "when that which is perfect is come" in the spiritual realm, that which is partial (limited or infantile) will be done away with (v. 10). Remember the Greek word *teleios* translates to "perfect" and can mean "complete, mature, or fully grown." The immature (childish) is put away when the mature comes. At this arrival of the "perfect," Paul later said that the corruptible puts on the cloak of the incorruptible, and we shall all be changed in a moment in the twinkling of an eye. When we see Him "face to face," we will put away all the foolishness of our flesh as a grown man puts away the foolish limitations of an infant. This thought should make us so humble.

No matter how much knowledge we attain in this corruptible life, we are still like an infant who cannot speak compared to the change that will occur when the perfect comes, and we meet the Lord Jesus face-to-face. Yes, it is humbling, and our flesh resists that. Even though there is a greater humbling on the horizon when the "perfect" comes, the final judgment, our spirits cry out: "Even so, come, Lord Jesus" (Rev. 22:20).

Chapter 6
Speaking Beforehand

There is an important truth concerning prophecy in the meaning of its name. As I said in the beginning, "prophecy" is translated from the Greek word *prophetes* and stems from *pro*, meaning "beforehand," and *phemi*, meaning "to tell." Thus, to prophesy is to "speak beforehand." I have often heard that a prophet was one who could foretell the future, and there are numerous examples of this in the Bible. Unlike the random or calculated predictions of soothsayers and for-tune-tellers, these prophets spoke under the influence of the Holy Spirit (2 Pet. 2:20–21), and thus, their prophecies always came true just as God spoke.

The apostle Peter, who was on the mountain of the Transfiguration and saw Jesus, Moses, and Elijah, and heard the Lord from heaven, wrote, "We have also *a more sure word of prophecy*; where unto ye do well that ye take heed" (2 Pet. 1:19, emphasis added). Furthermore, prophecy is directed solely by the Holy Spirit. "For the prophecy came not in old time by the will of man: *but holy men of God spake as they were moved by the Holy Ghost*" (2 Pet. 1:21, emphasis added). These predictions were not of man or the will of man but of the will of God by the power of His Spirit.

An example of such prophecy in the New Testament would be Acts 21:10–12, in which a prophet from Judea named Agabus foretold Paul's future arrest in Jerusalem and transfer to Rome. We know that this later came true. In addition, the New Testament gives much prophecy about the next appearance of Christ. It is difficult to understand the issues involved in such a cataclysmic event as the end of the world; however, Peter said it is a "sure" word, and it will come true whether or not we have understanding.

In the Old Testament, there were multiple prophets who foretold of the first advent of Jesus Christ. They prophesied where and how He would be born, as well as the events surrounding His death. In addition, these Old Testament prophets revealed much truth concerning the return of Christ for His bride at the end of the world. Other examples of prophecies that have been verified in history would include Nebuchadnezzar's dream in Daniel 2, which we previously examined. In fact, Daniel 7–11 reads much like any history book, yet it was written hundreds of years before those events came to pass.

How does revealing the future reveal the mysteries and knowledge of God? The answer is: they are one and the same.

Remember, in the future there exists a time when the "perfect" will come, and we have determined that the "perfect" is the Lord Jesus. This time is when He returns to meet His bride "face to face." At this time, there will be an end to sin. Prophecy and knowledge, which are currently partial in their nature, will be destroyed permanently. At this point, we will have full knowledge, just as Christ fully knows us now. This knowledge will be complete, experiential knowledge (denoted by the Greek word *epiginosko*). It is the intimate knowledge that a husband has of his wife when he meets her "face to face." Therefore, at the end of the age, when Christ takes His bride, all things will be revealed, and there will be no further need for prophecy. All history will come to pass by that time, and by that time, all vision and prophecy will have been fulfilled. There will be no more news concerning this man's world. All the mysteries of God will be revealed, and all His secrets and hidden wisdom will be exposed.

Now if, under the direction of the Holy Spirit, I reveal a secret or mystery of God before the "perfect" comes at the end of the age, then I have spoken before that time. In other words, I have spoken beforehand, foretold, or prophesied. That is where the word gets its origin and true meaning. When a child of God reveals a mystery of the kingdom of God before the time when full knowledge is present, then he has spoken beforehand, or prophesied. We must remember that this prophecy or foretelling of the mysteries is only partial and limited. The future is God's secret, which only He knows (Satan only makes good guesses). It is a mystery and is hidden from us at this point. At the end of the age, when the perfect is come, all history of man will be completed and revealed. To accurately foretell the future would be revealing the secrets or mysteries of God. Therefore, the aspect of prophecy that reveals the future is consistent with the definition of prophecy put forth in the first chapter.

The Light of Prophecy

Look again at 2 Peter 1:19: "We have also a more sure word of prophecy; whereunto ye do well that *ye take heed, as unto a light that shineth in a dark place,* until the day dawn, and the day star arise in your hearts" (emphasis added). Peter gave us a strong word, and we should listen and obey the prophetic word as God gives us revelation into His kingdom. Here Peter compared the prophetic word unto a light shining in the night until the sun rises the following morning. We understand that this light or lamp that shines would be partial; it would illuminate some of the dark but is just a temporary measure until the dawn approaches, and the sun rises. This verse again is a picture of the limited or partial aspects of prophecy until the "perfect" (Jesus) appears.

Throughout Scripture, the sun represents the Lord Jesus (Ps. 19:4–6; Rev. 1:16), and the moon represents His bride or His congregation (Gen. 37:9–10; Song of Solo 6:10).

Likewise, the dawn represents the end of the age when our Lord Jesus returns. While the light (from a lamp) shines in a dark place, it draws attention to itself but is very limited compared to the sun when it rises. In the same way, the prophetic word is quite stirring to our spirit, but it is only partial in nature. When the "perfect" comes, our partial understanding from prophecy will be like shining a flashlight when the sun rises. During a dark night, a flashlight is helpful and useful. It guides those who cannot see and keeps us from falling into a pit. But once the sun is risen, you can't even tell whether the flashlight is on. So it will be at the end of time when the Scripture says the sun will be dark, the moon will not give us light, and the stars will fall from the heavens at the entrance of the Lord Jesus (Matt. 24:29; Rev. 6:12).

We must have the "day star" alive in our hearts and let the penetrating light of His judgment search every aspect of our hearts and lives to see if any parts are not in submission to Him. We should allow the limited or partial aspects of prophecy, represented by the limited light available now, to examine our hearts and judge them by the Scriptures. In comparison to the light of the sun, there will be the final judgment when the penetrating light of the Lord Jesus exposes everything: "And the city had no need of the sun, neither of the moon, to shine in it: for the glory of God did lighten it, and the Lamb is the light [lamp] thereof" (Rev. 21:23).

Revealing the Heart

Stemming from this verse in 1 Peter, we need to address a third aspect or definition of prophecy. We have seen where prophecy is revealing the hidden secrets or mysteries of the knowledge of God and the mysteries or secrets of the future, but prophecy is also revealing the secrets of the heart of man. First Corinthians 14:24–25 says, "But if all prophesy, and there come in one that believeth not, or one unlearned, he is convinced of all, he is judged of all: *And thus are the secrets of his heart are made manifest*; and so falling down on his face he will worship God, and report that God is in you of a truth" (emphasis added). This verse states that there is an element of prophecy that reveals the heart of a man just as the light shines in a dark place.

The heart of a man is hidden from the eyes or the flesh of others, and only the Spirit of God can see the heart of a man: "The heart is deceitful above all things, and desperately wicked: who can know it? I the LORD search the heart, I try the reins, even to give every man according to his ways, and according to the fruit of his doings" (Jer. 17:9–10). When you and I look at people, we can examine only their external appearances and behavior, but God searches the heart. We can see only their actions, but God knows their motivations. It is the motivation or heart that determines the true source of the action, and unfortunately, our hearts are mostly deceived. The motivation of the Spirit is to serve others and draw little attention. Our flesh may serve others, but it usually does so to glorify itself or relieve guilt.

Since 1 Corinthians 14:24–25 refers to "the secrets of the heart," known only to the Spirit, then these secrets are secrets of God. In other words, the secrets of every man's heart are secrets of God. When a child of God, under the direction of the Holy Spirit, reveals the secrets of another's heart, he is revealing the secrets or mysteries of God, the way Nathan exposed David's secret sin. Only the Spirit of God through a prophet could do this. A prophet is prophesying when he is revealing the secrets or mysteries of another's heart. We all know at the end of the age when "that which is perfect is come," all knowledge will be revealed, and we will have to give an account for every idle word: "But I say unto you, That every idle word that men shall speak, they shall give account thereof in the day of judgment" (Matt. 12:36). Thus, all the evil secrets of our hearts will be revealed. These ugly truths or secrets of our hearts, which only God knows, will all be revealed and made manifest at the end of the age. Therefore, if a child of God, under the direction of the Holy Spirit, is able to reveal the secrets of another's heart now, he is speaking beforehand. He is revealing these secrets now, before the coming of that which is "perfect" at the end of the age. Thus, he is foretelling or prophesying.

Another picture of revealing the secrets of the heart is given in the parable of the sower (Matt. 13; Mark 4; Luke 8). In this parable, the soil represents the heart of man and holds the most important part of a plant—the roots. The health of a plant is determined mainly by its roots, just as the spiritual health of a child of God is determined by the condition of the heart. When we look at a plant, we can see only that which is above the ground, such as the stem, the leaves, the flower, and, hopefully, fruit. Scripture says we should be focused on fruit, something that is above the ground. We cannot look in the soil and cannot see the condition of the roots; we can see only the condition of the plant above the ground. In other words, we just see the outward part of the plant. Only the Spirit of God can see in the soil or the heart of man. For a man to see the secrets of another's heart, they must be revealed to him by the Holy Spirit as an aspect of prophecy.

In summary prophecy is speaking beforehand—more specifically, speaking before the end of the age when the "perfect" (Jesus) comes, and all is revealed. To reveal the mysteries concerning the kingdom of God before this event would be to speak beforehand or to prophesy. Paul defined it as revealing the mysteries and knowledge of God, and these secrets may be contained in the parables of Jesus, the writings of Paul, or other Scriptures. The secrets of God also contain the future and even the hearts of men. To reveal these secrets beforehand is the definition of prophecy.

Chapter 7
The True Riches

Several years ago, I was traveling with Dr. M. A. Thomas, from Kota, India–a man from whom I have learned so much; and, as always, I was pestering him with multiple questions about the Scriptures. When I asked him about a "picture" that I saw in the Gospel of John, he abruptly said, "You have insight!" He did not mention terms such as *prophecy, revelation,* or *illumination.* He referred to seeing this hidden (secret) picture contained within the Scripture as receiving "insight" from the Spirit of God. He said these insights are the true riches of the kingdom of God.

Next, he quoted Luke 16:10–13, where Jesus said:

> He that is faithful in that which is least is faithful also in much: and he that is unjust in the least is unjust also in much. *If therefore ye have not been faithful in the unrighteous mammon* [money or

wealth], *who will commit to your trust the true
riches?* And if ye have not been faithful in that
which is another man's, who shall give you that
which is your own? No servant can serve two
masters: for either he will hate the one, and love
the other; or else he will hold to the one, and
despise the other. Ye cannot serve God and
mammon. (emphasis added)

I already understood from verse 10 that whoever stole little
amounts would also steal large amounts, if the risks of being
caught were the same. I also knew that stealing was the same,
whether it was one dollar or a thousand; because the same
evil heart, which does not trust God but trusts in the stolen
money, dictates it.

However, verse 11 was quite new to me: "If therefore you
have not been faithful in the unrighteous mammon, who will
commit to your trust the true riches?" Mammon is actually
the transliterated Greek word *mammonas,* meaning "wealth,
possessions, money, and the power associated with such
things." So if you are not faithful in the managing of unrighteous or worldly riches, then who will trust you with these
"true riches" that obviously come from God? God judges the
hearts of all men (1 Chron. 28:9; 1 Sam. 16:7; 1 Kings 8:39;
Luke 16:15), and there are few greater tests or temptations of
our hearts than money and power. In fact, a common practice in training children or even employees is to entrust (test)

them first with things of lesser value before risking those things that are greatly appraised. If a child cannot manage the possessions and property of his parents, why should he receive an inheritance just to squander? Until we can manage and view wealth and money with a pure heart toward God, He will not entrust to us His valuables or "true riches."

Prophecy Produces the "True Riches"

"True riches" certainly are not money and power, for Jesus said, "God knoweth your hearts: for that which is highly esteemed among men [money, possessions, and power] is abomination in the sight of God" (Luke 16:15). Dr. Thomas described these "true riches" as insight from Scripture, or the ability to see the picture (hidden meaning) God intended. The Scriptures refer to these hidden truths as the mysteries of God, and receiving insight into these mysteries is revelation. The true riches of the kingdom of God are knowledge of Him. They are hidden "treasures" buried within the Scriptures, which can be uncovered or unveiled only by the Spirit. It is the manifestation of prophecy that reveals these "true riches" of God's kingdom.

Though the "treasures" of eternity are not the mammon of this world, they are pictured as such in Scripture (Rev. 3:18). The knowledge of God is a bottomless mine shaft covered in gold, silver, and precious stones. Just as we test gold and silver in the refining fire (1 Cor. 3:12–14), revelation must be tested against Scripture (Acts 17:11) as well as with other saints (1 Cor. 14:29). Just as the refining fire reveals impurities in the precious metals, the Scriptures, as well as the brethren, help reveal impurities in our revelations. And like gems and precious metals, truth is a treasure because it is so rare.

The "true riches" are wisdom and knowledge of God, and they are far beyond what man can see on his own: *"O the depth of the riches both of the wisdom and knowledge of God!* how unsearchable are his judgments, and his ways past finding out! For who hath known the mind of the Lord? or who hath been his counsellor?" (Rom. 11:33–34, emphasis added) Oh, the mysteries and secrets of God, known as His riches, are so deep! They do not lie on the surface where any eye can see or any ear can hear, but they are deep, covered by layers of veils. These veils must be removed before the wisdom or mysteries are revealed. Just as Paul had the scales fall from his eyes (Acts 9:18), we have veils over ours that must be removed. No one can know the mind of the Lord unless God chooses to reveal His thoughts to that person. The Lord needs no counselor.

In Paul's letter to the Ephesians, he made several references to the riches of God being the mysteries or hidden secrets of His knowledge:

> Unto me [Paul], who am less than the least of all
> saints, is this grace given, that *I should preach*

*among the Gentiles the unsearchable riches of
Christ; And to make all men see what is the fellowship of the mystery, which from the beginning of the
world hath been hid in God,* who created all things
by Jesus Christ: To the intent that now unto the
principalities and powers in heavenly places might
be known by the church the manifold wisdom of
God, According to the eternal purpose which he
purposed in Christ Jesus our Lord. (Eph. 3:8–11,
emphasis added)

It was only by the grace of God that Paul was able to speak
and reveal to the Gentiles those "unsearchable riches of
Christ" (v. 8). It was only by the power of the Holy Spirit
that Paul was able to see these unsearchable truths called
"riches" and make known to man the mysteries, that have
been hidden in Christ since the beginning of the world. As
verse 10 suggests, God's intent was that the bride of Christ
(through the Holy Spirit) would know His wisdom.

Hidden in Christ

Furthermore, in verse 11, Paul said that it is God's eternal
purpose and intention that He placed (hid) in Jesus Christ.
In other words, all the mysteries and knowledge of God are
hidden in Jesus Christ. He is our only Advocate or Intermediary

with the Father, and though many may claim to know God in a relationship, it is impossible to know the Creator except through Jesus Christ. Jesus said, "I am the way, the truth, and the life: *no man cometh unto the Father, but by me*" (John 14:6, emphasis added). Luke wrote in Acts 4:12, "There is none other name [than Jesus] under heaven given among men, whereby we must be saved." Also, later Paul proclaimed in 1 Timothy 2:5, "For there is one God, and one mediator between God and men, the man Christ Jesus." As stated in Ephesians 3:9, "*the mystery, which from the beginning of the world hath been hid in God, who created all things by Jesus Christ*" (emphasis added), it is Jesus Christ who created the world, and before He created it, all the secrets, wisdom, and power of God were hidden in Him.

If God's intent is that the bride of Christ know the complete or "manifold wisdom of God" (Eph. 3:10), and that wisdom is hidden in Jesus Christ, then we (the bride) are to know Jesus (wisdom) completely. Then the mystery of God will be completed when we see Jesus "face to face." At that time, we will know Him fully (completely), just as He knows us fully. Remember, this full or complete knowledge is signified by the Greek word *epiginosko* and represents the secret knowledge completely exposed between a husband and bride.

God's intent is that the bride (the church) would completely know Jesus. This will occur when the "perfect" comes. Remember, *teleios* translates as "perfect" and means complete. All that is hidden in Christ (knowledge) will be completely and fully ours when He returns for His bride (us). We must not be a bride who tries to figure her Husband out with her intellect or cunning alone. We must be the humble, reserved, faithful, and submissive bride of another time who was created to serve the Husband (Gen. 2:20). This is the bride in whom the Husband confides, and this is the bride to whom the Husband reveals His secrets. These brides are the wise virgins (Matt. 25:1–13) whom the Husband will take with Him.

Again, these secrets are shared only with those who are in a close relationship with the Lord:

> And he said unto them, *Unto you it is given to know the mysteries of the kingdom of God: but unto them that are without, all these things are done in parables.* That seeing they may see, and not perceive; and hearing they may hear, and not understand; lest at any time they should be converted, and their sins should be forgiven them. (Mark 4:11–12, emphasis added)

Many heard Jesus share the parables, but only a few heard the interpretation or the explaining of parables. Only those close to the Lord in an intimate relationship (the disciples and others following Him closely) would see the mysteries.

As we discussed earlier, prophecy can be represented as a light shining in darkness to reveal what is hidden. Therefore, insight, revelation, and prophecy can also be described as *enlightenment* or *illumination*. Look again at Ephesians 3:9 where Paul said, "And to make all men see what is the fellowship of the mystery ..." The phrase "to make all men see" is translated from the Greek word *photiso*, meaning "light." A more accurate translation would read "to enlighten, to shine light upon, or to bring to light the fellowship of the mystery." A more literal rendering of verses 8 and 9 might state that Paul was "given power or favor to share the good news of the unsearchable riches of Christ *by illuminating or revealing this secret fellowship with Christ which was hidden by God when the world was created*." Another interesting aspect of this passage is the word "fellowship" in verse 9. It is translated from the Greek word *koinonia* and represents a sharing-type relationship and is often translated "communion." This communion represents the relationship between fellow believers as well as the child of God with the Lord Jesus. Again, verse 9 might be better translated "to enlighten or reveal to all men the secrets, which are shared with us by the Lord Jesus (or by other believers) but yet are unsearchable without the Holy Spirit."

Later in this same chapter, Paul again described the riches of God as knowledge of Him through Christ:

> That he would grant you, *according to the riches of his glory*, to be strengthened with might by his Spirit in the inner man; *That Christ may dwell in your hearts by faith*; that ye, being rooted and

grounded in love, May be able to comprehend
with all saints what is the breadth, and length,
and depth, and height; And to know the love of
Christ, which passeth knowledge, *that ye might be*
filled with all the fulness of God. (Eph. 3:16–19,
emphasis added)

Paul desired that God would give us His riches to strengthen
our inner man (v. 16). And what are His riches? They are
knowledge of Him revealed through prophecy, and are given
to strengthen our inner man; therefore, prophecy must
strengthen or build up our inner man. Just as an earthly
father would use his wealth to strengthen or give his children
advantage, our heavenly Father uses His riches (wisdom) to
benefit us spiritually. Any understanding we have is according
to His riches, which is knowledge of Him.

In his letters to the Colossians, Paul referred to the riches
of God being knowledge of Him several times:

Whereof I am made a minister [servant], according to the dispensation [stewardship] of God
which is given to me for you, to fulfil the word of
God; *Even the mystery which hath been hid from*
ages and from generations, but now is made mani-
fest to his saints: To whom God would make known
what is the riches of the glory of this mystery among
the Gentiles; which is Christ in you, the hope of
glory. (Col. 1:25–27, emphasis added)

Here again the riches of the glory of God are the mystery, which has been hidden from the beginning of the world but has now been made known to His bride (the saints, or the "true" church). These secrets were hidden in Christ before He created the world, and today are revealed to those who are intimate with Him. A few verses later, Paul again spoke of the riches of God stemming from His secrets: "That their hearts might be comforted, being knit together in love, and *unto all riches of the full assurance of understanding, to the acknowledgement of the mystery of God, and of the Father, and of Christ; In whom are hid all the treasures of wisdom and knowledge*" (Col. 2:2–3, emphasis added). Again we see the "riches" of God are the "full assurance of understanding" of the secrets of God (v. 2). Actually, verse 2 divides the mystery of God into that of the Father and of Christ, and it is in Christ where all the treasures of the kingdom of God are hidden. These treasures of the kingdom of God are wisdom and knowledge (verse 3), which we receive today through prophecy or revelation.

In the next chapter of Colossians, Paul again pointed to the wisdom or knowledge of God being His riches: "Let the word of Christ *dwell in you richly* in all wisdom" (Col. 3:16, emphasis added). The word "richly" is the same Greek word that is translated "riches," so the Word of Christ should dwell in us as riches. The riches of the kingdom of God do not dwell on our outside as clothing, jewelry, or material possessions. They dwell in us. The riches of the kingdom of God

71

dwell in the hearts of the children of God in the form of knowledge and wisdom. These can come only from God and are given to us by His Spirit. Remember, these riches are hidden in Christ, and if Christ is in us, then these secrets can dwell in us. We must be in Christ, for if we do not have a proper perspective on the riches of this world, why would God entrust to us the riches of the "world to come"?

Seek the True

Back in Luke 16:11, where we started our discussion of the "true riches" of God, we should note that the word "riches" does not actually occur in the Greek but is merely implied. This verse may also be translated as: "If one is untrustworthy with unrighteous material riches, who will commit into his trust the true?" There are false riches, which are material possessions of this world, and there are the true riches or secrets of the kingdom of God. Even though the word "riches" does not actually occur in the Greek following the word "true," the translation we are using is probably accurate because *riches* is clearly implied in this verse. But we should examine this further.

The Greek word translated as "true" in this verse is *alethinos*, meaning "genuine or real." We mentioned there are the false or deceiving riches of this world, and there are the "true riches" or the secrets of the kingdom of God, which are hidden in Christ Jesus. There is the "false bread" that the Jews ate in the wilderness (manna), and there is the "true bread from heaven":

"Then Jesus said unto them, Verily, verily, I say unto you, Moses gave you not that bread from heaven; but my Father giveth you the *true bread* from heaven. For the bread of God is he [Jesus] which cometh down from heaven, and giveth life unto the world" (John 6:32–33, emphasis added). In the same way, there is the vine in the vineyard producing fruit, and then there is the "true vine" (John 15:1) who is Jesus. There is the tabernacle (temporary dwelling of God) the Jews built in the wilderness, and then there is the "true tabernacle, which the Lord pitched, and not man" (Heb. 8:2). There was the holy place in the tabernacle and temple of the Jews, and then there is the true holy place in heaven itself in the presence of God: "For Christ is not entered into the holy places made with hands, which are the figures of the true; but into heaven itself, now to appear in the presence of God for us" (Heb. 9:24). God used bread, a vine, and the tabernacle of the Jews to teach or foretell of the *true* that is in heaven. Likewise, the mammon (wealth) of this world is a picture of the "true riches," which is knowledge of Him.

God has made Himself known to man through creation as well as Scripture (Rom. 1:20). In addition, the experiences of the Jews also give us insight into the secrets of God, for these events happened as examples for us (1 Cor. 10:6,11). Likewise, the vine was created to teach and reveal the secrets of the "true vine," Jesus. The manna, which came from heaven and appeared in the wilderness for the Jews to eat, was a picture of the "true bread" that came from heaven,

Christ Jesus. The tabernacle, which the Jews built and moved as the cloud moved before them, was a picture of the true tabernacle of God, Christ Jesus. All these are mere symbols of the genuine or true—Christ Jesus.

Remember, all the secrets of the kingdom of God are hidden in Jesus and concern Him. He is the Secret of God, and it is Christ Jesus who has restored the relationship or fellowship with God that was lost in the Garden of Eden. It is in these parables, allegories, pictures, or mysteries that God hid the knowledge of Himself through Christ before the foundation of the world. In Ezekiel 16:10–13, God adorned His bride, Israel, with all the precious things of this world as a symbol of how He had spiritually blessed His people. In the New Testament we have seen that He adorns the bride of Christ with His mysteries, for these are the true riches in His kingdom.

Chapter 8
Stewards of the
Mysteries of God

It is interesting that these "true riches" or secrets of the kingdom are entrusted to us (Luke 16:11). Usually possessions or
riches are entrusted to a steward who also manages the
wealthy person's house. A steward, often a slave himself, would
manage the domestic affairs of the whole household and often
would supervise other slaves or servants, and even children.
Stewards were often employed or paid to manage a household
or sometimes an entire city (Rom. 16:23). A steward was
expected to manage his master's most prized possessions in the
same manner that the master would manage them.

A steward is different from a servant in that a steward
has managerial responsibilities; a slave or servant would
merely follow instructions. In a household during biblical
times, a servant who proved trustworthy and obedient to all
the lord or master commanded of him would soon be pro-

moted and be given stewardship. The master would choose as stewards only those who reflected his character and could be trusted to carry on his affairs in a manner that benefited him. The steward did not own or receive income from those possessions, but he was merely paid to manage them according to the master's will.

Many Christians understand the concept of stewardship regarding the material possessions that God has given us. Everything we have belongs to and comes from God, and we are merely to manage those possessions as He desires. In order to manage His possessions as He desires, we must first hear and know His instructions. In addition, we must know the heart of the Master as well as His intentions. This is why "true" discipleship is just learning to hear His voice. It is the basis of all our experience in the Christian life. Even prayer should be listening; why does God always have to hear our voices when He knows our hearts? We must hear His voice. There is no way to be obedient without first hearing His voice. In fact, the Hebrew word *shama* (or *shema*) is translated as "hear" as well as "obey" throughout the Old Testament. My children, in all their effort, cannot do what I desire unless they first sit and listen to my desires. In the same way, stewards must focus on hearing the Master and waiting for Him to speak.

Yes, we are stewards of the material possessions that God has given us, but even more, we are stewards of His "true riches" or mysteries. Paul wrote, "Let a man so account of us, as of the ministers [under servants] of Christ, and *stewards of the mysteries of God.* Moreover it is required in stewards, that a man be found faithful"(1 Cor. 4:1–2, emphasis added). We are to be stewards or managers of the secrets of the kingdom of God.

We Are Under Servants of Christ

This intimate knowledge revealed through a relationship is private and is not to be told to a "talebearer" (Prov. 11:13). These secrets are to be shared with those God desires and shared in His timing. As the Spirit leads us, we should share them with those whom God has deemed ready to hear. Otherwise we are throwing our "pearls before swine" (Matt. 7:6). Yet, "a man [must] be found faithful," before he can be a steward, so we must first be faithful servants before we can be stewards (1 Cor. 4:2). Even though Paul said that we all may prophesy (1 Cor. 14:31), God will entrust His greatest "riches" and deepest secrets to those whose hearts have been tested and found faithful. This is the heart that seeks only the will of the Master. This is the heart of a servant who will become a steward.

As an aside, we should note that in 1 Corinthians 4:1, the phrase "the ministers of Christ" is literally, in Greek, "the under servants of Christ." The Greek word translated "ministers" in verse 1 is *huperetes,* which comes from *hupo,* meaning "under or beneath" and *eretes,* referring to "a rower." The word stems from naval vocabulary at that time and referred to the slaves who rowed the ships of war. These slaves were often prisoners and were bought and sold at the captain's wishes. *Huperetes* refers to the lowest of the rowers, or the lowest of the low. The word "minister" in our translations is often translated from the Greek word *diakonos*, meaning "a servant, specifically one who would wait tables." It is where we get our English word *deacon*. Both *huperetes* and *diakonos* imply "a lowly servant." Whether you are the lowest rower on a ship or waiting tables at a feast while the guests enjoy the meal, it is an occupation of low position. The intent of the authors (under the guidance of the Holy Spirit) was that of service from a humble, low position.

If I told you that I wanted to serve you, you would visualize me as being your subordinate and beneath you. It even has an air of my not being as "good" as you, and I would be beneath you in service. This is one aspect of why Jesus said the "first shall be last; and the last shall be first" (Matt. 19:30). The Lord also said that he who wants to be the chief must become the servant of all (Luke 22:26). Accomplishing this requires complete humility and the deaths of our wills, which desire to be served in order to acquire the chief position, and to be first among the many.

Unfortunately, our translations are misleading by using the word "minister" in these verses. In our culture today, the word "minister" has little to do with the concept of the lowest rower or the least waiter. Some of the highest offices in government carry the title of minister, such as the minister of defense. If someone said that he was going to minister to you, it might suggest a sense of spiritual superiority. Implied in this statement is that he is of a higher spiritual status and possesses ability or information that can elevate you to "his level." Sadly, this is often carried into institutional forms of church where a minister or ministers are usually in authority over others in the congregation. In addition, deacons are often in positions of authority as well, and are not lowly servants. Although 1 Timothy 3:10 mentions "the office of a deacon," the word "office" does not occur in the Greek. This is just one example of a translation bias.

In contrast, the scriptural concept of these words is the person who would merely clean up after a meal or sweep the floor after a meeting. We must have…humble hearts of servants and actually serve others, instead of "ministering" to them. We must be humble, broken servants who are faithful in the least of the Master's orders before we can be stewards: "*He that is faithful in that which is least is faithful also in much*; and he that is unjust in the least is unjust also in much. If therefore ye have not been faithful in the unrighteous mammon, who will commit to your trust the true riches?" (Luke 16:10–11, emphasis added) I personally receive more revelation when doing menial tasks than when doing important ones.

As we examine these verses from Luke, what does the Lord mean by "that which is least"? The least of things is clearly the material possessions (unrighteous mammon) of this world. If we cannot be faithful in managing the things that will burn at the end of the age, why would God entrust to us the true riches of His eternal nature? Before we can see the mysteries of the kingdom of God, we must have a proper attitude toward material possessions.

The Heart of a Steward

This proper attitude all stems from our hearts. We must have meek or humble hearts: "Blessed are the meek: for they shall inherit the earth" (Matt. 5:5). We must seek to serve the lowest of the low people: "And the King shall answer and say unto them, Verily I say unto you, *Inasmuch as ye have done it unto one of the least of these my brethren, ye have done it unto me*" (Matt. 25:40, emphasis added). We must be careful never to give to or treat the wealthy above the low, for this would be disobedient to God (James 2:2–9). In fact, Scripture warns of giving to the rich (to a person or an organization) (Prov. 22:16). When we give to someone who is wealthy or of means, it is often our flesh that gives, trying to gain influence with them. This is what the wicked steward was doing in Luke 16:1–9. The exception may be giving out of thankfulness to a person who has taught you of God (Gal. 6:6).

What God desires is a humble, broken heart willing to serve the least of these. Humble, faithful servants are the ones He will choose as His stewards. Joseph was chosen as a steward not because of his brilliance but because of his faithfulness and humility. God gave both Joseph and Moses great ability, but first, each had to endure years of performing the most menial tasks before being appointed over whole kingdoms: "He that is faithful in that which is least is faithful also in much" (Luke 16:10).

The Lord Jesus best described the responsibility of stewardship in Luke 12:40–49:

> Be ye therefore ready also: for the Son of man
> cometh at an hour when ye think not. Then
> Peter said unto him, Lord, speakest thou this
> parable unto us, or even to all? *And the Lord said,*
> *Who then is that faithful and wise steward whom*
> *his lord shall make ruler over his household, to give*
> *them their portion of meat in due season? Blessed is*
> *that servant, whom his lord when he cometh shall*
> *find so doing.* Of a truth I say unto you, that he
> will make him ruler over all that he hath. But
> and if that servant say in his heart, My lord
> delayeth his coming; and shall begin to beat the
> menservants and maidens, and to eat and drink,
> and to be drunken; The lord of that servant will
> come in a day when he looketh not for him, and
> at an hour when he is not aware, and will cut
> him in sunder, and will appoint him his portion
> with the unbelievers. And that servant, which
> knew his lord's will, and prepared not himself,

neither did according to his will, shall be beaten
with many stripes. But he that knew not, and
did commit things worthy of stripes, shall be
beaten with few stripes. For unto whomsoever
much is given, of him shall be much required:
and to whom men have committed much, of
him they will ask the more. *I am come to send
fire on the earth; and what will I, if it be already
kindled*? (emphasis added)

We often give because we fear man and desire the things of
men instead of the things of God. I have seen so many
Christian leaders cater to wealthy church members or ministry supporters thinking how the kingdom of God could
benefit from the wealthy person's money. God already has all
the money in the world; He does not need it from anyone!
What He lacks are faithful servants who first can be stewards
of the unrighteous mammon (money), and then become
stewards of His mysteries. He owns all our possessions any-
way. At the end of the age, He will come and take them back
by force merely to throw them in a fire. Material riches are of
little value to God.

Stewards Share

We should examine Luke 12:48 in more detail: "For unto
whomsoever much is given, of him shall be much required:

and to whom men have committed much, of him they will ask the more." It is clear that when a master entrusts possessions to a steward, he expects a return on his investment. The greater the trust or the possessions managed, the greater the expectation of the return as Jesus taught in the parable of the talents (Matt. 25:14–30). Our flesh tends to think in terms of material possessions, but these passages apply as well to the "true riches" or secrets of God's kingdom. The more intimate knowledge that we receive, the more that is expected of us as stewards of these secrets.

We are to share the material possessions with those who would be considered "the least of these," specifically, widows and orphans (James 1:27). In the same way, we are to share His mysteries and secrets with "the least of these" as well, those who are not "puffed up" with pride or arrogance of knowledge, and those who are not seeking a sign or to have their stomachs filled like the Jews of Jesus' time (John 6:26). It is those of a humble heart who are poor in spirit who are the faithful and obedient slaves of the Master. It is these faithful few to whom God will reveal His secrets. It is these few who will become wise stewards: "Blessed are the poor in spirit: for theirs is the kingdom of heaven" (Matt. 5:3).

Many times when a Christian speaks in a group, we call it *sharing*. This term *sharing* is quite accurate scripturally. As we receive the "true riches" of the kingdom of God, we are to share them with others just as we are to share our material blessings. Sharing the "true riches" is sharing the secrets of

God. In many Christian assemblies, the majority of "sharing" presents itself as personal experiences, prayer requests, and prearranged lessons or sermons, but this may not be the Lord's intention.

In 1 Corinthians 14:26–37, Paul instructed us how to have an assembly or church meeting. Though there was a time when Paul stated that he spoke of himself, this was not that time. In fact, Paul gave this passage more authority than the rest of his letters because at the conclusion of this passage, Paul said, "If any man think himself to be a prophet, or spiritual, let him acknowledge *that the things that I write unto you are the commandments of the Lord*" (v. 37, emphasis added). Paul clearly stated that you may think you have some special knowledge or prophecy that differs, but these instructions on how to meet are commandments of the Lord. This is the only instance in which Paul used such strong, authoritative words in any of his writings. If we are to follow any of Paul's instructions, should we not begin with those deemed the "commandments of the Lord"? When we meet today, are we following the traditions of men, or the "commandments of the Lord"?

In these instructions (commandments), the Lord desires at least two or three to share secrets or mysteries of the Lord (v. 29), which we know as prophecy. In fact, all the men present may share a revelation if God so desires (v. 31). Why does God desire different individuals to share in a meeting? Why does He restrict women from speaking in the assembly

(vv. 34–35)? I have some ideas, but you will have to ask the Master because they are His commandments.

Finally, let us look again at Luke 12:42: "And the Lord said, Who then is that faithful and wise steward, whom his lord shall make ruler over his household, to give them their portion of meat in due season?" A faithful and wise steward is to provide the other servants with their "portion [share] of meat" at the right time. This phrase is translated from the Greek word *sitometrion* and means "a measure or share of grain." The word "meat" is misleading in our modern vernacular. This picture obviously has a physical fulfillment in that we are stewards of the material possessions God gives us. We are to provide for (share with) those who are weak (Acts 20:34–35), as well as the widows and orphans (James 1:27). As wise and faithful stewards of the material blessing, we are to give others their portion or share at the proper time (as determined by the Holy Spirit).

In similar fashion, this parable has a spiritual fulfillment as well. As stewards of the true riches or secret knowledge of the kingdom of God, we are to share these with others as the Spirit leads. Again, as stewards, we are "to give them their portion [share] of meat in due season" (Luke 12:42). We are not to give all we are entrusted with, but we are to share the Lord's secrets according to His will. This is how a steward is to operate. In the spiritual fulfillment of this parable, the steward is a prophet. Yet in the kingdom of God, "ye may all prophesy one by one, that all may learn, and all may be comforted" (1 Cor. 14:31). God desires that we all grow in faith to become stewards and share His mysteries as well as His material goods. But unlike mystery religions, which require a special knowledge to understand their principles, Christianity's mysteries are shared based on the state of one's heart.

Chapter 9
The Purpose of Prophecy

As we have seen, the mysteries of God are His "true riches" that are hidden in Christ Jesus and revealed only to those in a close and intimate relationship with Him. In other words, only the obedient and faithful steward will be entrusted with the mysteries of the kingdom of God. But, you may ask, what is the purpose of prophecy and knowing these mysteries? Is it just vain knowledge of the prideful heart that wants to know everyone's secrets? Certainly the material blessings from the unrighteous mammon of this world have much practical application in feeding the hungry, clothing the naked, and sheltering the homeless, but what is the value in these true riches? What practical value is there in knowing the mysteries and knowledge of God? Why does He place them above all material things?

Paul answered these questions concisely in a verse we examined earlier: "But he that prophesieth speaketh unto men to *edification, and exhortation, and comfort*" (1 Cor. 14:3, emphasis added). Prophecy edifies (builds up), exhorts, and comforts the body of Christ: "He that speaketh in an unknown tongue edifieth [only] himself; but he that prophesieth edifieth the [whole] church" (1 Cor. 14:4). Prophecy should be selfless in that it builds up, exhorts, and comforts others (as well as oneself). It has little practical application to the flesh, but it possesses great value for the Spirit. It is a manifestation of the Spirit given that we might "*be strengthened with might by His Spirit in the inner man*; That Christ may dwell in your hearts by faith; that ye, being rooted and grounded in love, *May be able to comprehend* with all saints what is the breadth, and length, and depth, and height; And to know the love of Christ, which passeth knowledge, that ye might be filled with all the fulness of God" (Eph. 3:16–19, emphasis added).

Edification

As to these three purposes of prophecy, let us first look at edification. The Greek word translated "edification" is *oikodome*, meaning "the act or process of building or a building up," and it specifically refers to the building of a house. *Oikodome* comes from *oikos*, meaning "house," and *doma*, meaning "to build." Thus, edification means "a building up, strengthening, or growing process" and is pictured by building a house. In 1 Corinthians 3:10–13, Paul said:

> According to the grace of God which is given
> unto me, *as a wise masterbuilder, I have laid the*
> *foundation, and another buildeth thereon.* But let
> every man take heed how he buildeth thereupon.
> For other foundation can no man lay than that is
> laid, which is Jesus Christ. Now if any man build
> upon this foundation *gold, silver, precious stones,*
> wood, hay, stubble; Every man's work shall be
> made manifest: for *the day shall declare it, because it*
> *shall be revealed by fire*; and the fire shall try every
> man's work of what sort it is. (emphasis added)

Notice that the gold, silver, and precious stones will pass
through the fire on the last day and enter into eternity, for
these are the true riches of God. They are eternal and invisible
to the eyes of most men. The wood, hay, and stubble are the
foolish "fables," teachings, and traditions of men that will
burn as all our material possessions will by the refining fire of
God (v. 13) on the last day. The house is only as stable as the
foundation—as with the importance of building on rock versus sand, detailed in Matthew 7:24–27—and the building
materials used (gold, silver, and precious stones versus wood,
hay, and stubble).

In these verses, Paul was referring to the building up of
believers or children of God within the body of Christ. Many
would think that this building up has to do with the size or
the number in the body, but that is not true. Edification

refers to building the individuals within the body. The Greek word *oikodome* has nothing to do with building a number of houses but refers to building a single house at a time. This building up is clearly a growth in faith, not numbers.

Are we like Peter, who desired nothing more than to know Christ in a more intimate way so that He would reveal more of the secrets of the kingdom of God to him? Or are we like Judas, who on the outside appeared interested but inwardly wanted only to carry the "money bag" so he could steal from it as he desired, eventually betraying the Lord for thirty pieces of silver? Are we like Mary, who did the "best thing" by sitting at the Master's feet, enjoying His company, hearing His voice, and receiving His wisdom? Or are we like Martha, who desired to feed everyone and worried about what people thought of her housekeeping and cooking instead of seeking to spend time with the Lord Jesus? While Martha appeared to have a relationship with Jesus, deep down her heart wanted the approval of men. She called herself a disciple of the Lord, but she was more concerned about what she did out of her own understanding than spending time with and learning directly from Jesus, which is why she is a true mirror for many religious persons today.

In contrast, Mary ignored all the work and what people thought about her; she just wanted to hear the voice of the Lord. We must hear His voice and receive His instructions before we can do His work. Otherwise we are just like Martha, who did what *she* thought was right or good. So many today are doing all kinds of ministry and church work in the name of Jesus either to meet some need within themselves or because they are concerned about their witness and looking good before men. Like Martha, they often neglect to do that which is most important. We were created to spend time with Him. We were created not primarily to do good work but to be in a relationship with the Creator. Good works then must follow the relationship and be a result of hearing His voice. Otherwise, those works are mere religion.

In order for an individual to be edified or built up, he must first have a foundation already laid, and that foundation is Jesus Christ. Paul laid the foundations (planted the seed), and this building process is in individual believers: "But let every man take heed how he buildeth thereupon" (1 Cor. 3:10). This "building" should not be confused with adding numbers to the church, or multiplying. This building up is increasing in faith or ability to trust God. Our spiritual problems always stem from not trusting God, which is a lack of faith. All sin comes from not trusting God (Rom. 14:23). It is only by faith that we please God (Heb. 11:6). We are to grow in faith (2 Thess. 1:3), and growing is building (or *oikodome*) our faith. Faith comes from hearing His voice (Rom. 10:17). This is edification, and this is a purpose of prophecy. Instead of listening to stories or "fables" (1 Tim. 1:4), we need to hear from God through prophecy, and this builds our faith.

Thus, edification of the body is not just the building up, but it is a building up using the right materials, which are the true riches of the kingdom of God. The house that we build through the process of edification shall be full of the riches or hidden secrets of the kingdom of God: "In the house of the righteous is much treasure" (Prov. 15:6); "There is treasure to be desired and oil in the dwelling [house] of the wise" (Prov. 21:20). The treasure of the Lord is knowledge of Him: "Through wisdom is an house builded; and by understanding it is established: And by knowledge shall the chambers be filled with all precious and pleasant riches" (Prov. 24:3–4). This passage strongly supports, as we have seen, that edification is pictured as building a house. It is built by wisdom and established with a foundation by understanding. The rooms "will be filled with all precious and pleasant riches" by knowledge. Again, it is the knowledge of God that forms the true and "pleasant" riches of His kingdom.

The foundational secret on which we build our house is that we must die (John 12:24–25). Our souls or wills must be denied, and we must be crucified with Christ (Gal. 2:20). *Once we have understanding of this secret, then the foundation of Christ is laid within us, and this foundation stone is a gravestone.* When we deny our souls (Mark 8:35), we cease from building our own kingdoms and lay the foundation to build the kingdom of God within us. This is how "by understanding it [our house] is established" (Prov. 24:3). Once the foundation is laid, the house is then built by the wisdom that comes from God. The rooms are filled with the "true riches," which come from prophecy.

If understanding the secret of God is the foundation, then fear is digging the foundation. This whole foundation process begins with fear. All the riches of God stem from fear of Him: "The fear of the LORD is the beginning of knowledge" (Prov. 1:7). This wisdom and knowledge are God's "true riches" that he gives to those who fear Him: "*The secret of the LORD is with them that fear Him; and he will shew them His covenant*" (Ps. 25:14, emphasis added). The fear of the Lord is His treasure as well: "And wisdom and knowledge shall be the stability of thy times, and strength of salvation: *the fear of the LORD is his treasure*"(Isa. 33:6, emphasis added). The fear of the Lord is such a fantastic and wonderful treasure. Martin Luther started the Reformation in the sixteenth century based on his fear of God. It is when we are in fear of God that we have no fear of man and, therefore, have peace. When we fear man, we do not fear God and, therefore, can be swayed and moved about by the "waves" of men's opinions. When we fear the Lord and seek only to please Him, then we will not worry what man thinks of us, for that matters little if we are pleasing to our Father in heaven. Conversely, if we are not pleasing to our Father, then it matters not how well men think of us, for there will be no peace in our inward man, only an outward pride and temporary security from the opinion of men.

Edification, or building of our own house, begins with fear of God, and is accomplished by prophecy. This knowledge of the kingdom of God causes us to grow in faith and fills the rooms of our house with the "true riches." These are the intimate secrets God shares with those who have made covenant with Him. This whole process begins with fear.

Exhortation

The second purpose of prophecy, from 1 Corinthians 14:3, is "exhortation", translated from the Greek word *paraklesis*. It is the feminine noun from *parakaleo*. In most English New Testaments *paraklesis* is translated as "consolation" and occasionally as "exhortation". It comes from *para*, meaning "to the side or against," and *kaleo*, meaning "to call." In other words, it means "to call one alongside," usually for the purpose of aid, comfort, or encouragement. Exhortation is actually a very difficult word to define. There is a sense of comfort and consolation that we receive with prophecy, for seeing God's mysteries strengthens our relationship with Him. However, there appears to be more to the definition.

It is interesting that whereas the feminine noun *paraklesis* is translated "exhortation", the masculine noun *parakleetos* is translated "Comforter", referring to the Holy Spirit (John 16:7). Greek is such an explicit language that the gender of the word is even important. If the masculine noun refers to the Holy Spirit, then instead of Comforter, the Holy Spirit could be called the Exhorter. The masculine form, *parakleetos*, refers to exhortation or comfort provided by the

94

Husband (God) while the feminine word, *paraklesis*, is comfort from the bride of Christ. This feminine bride exhorts through prophecy. Both of these words come from *parakaleo*, which is translated "comfort" (resulting from prophecy) in 1 Corinthians 14:31. However, *parakaleo* is often translated "beseech", suggesting a strong warning or admonishment. Therefore, "calling to one's side" may imply a warning. It appears that beseeching or warning is what Paul most likely intended in the use of *paraklesis* in 1 Corinthians 14:3.

Jesus said that when the Comforter (*parakleetos*) comes into the world, He will convict the world of sin: "And when he [Comforter] is come, he will reprove [convict] the world of sin, and of righteousness, and of judgment" (John 16:8). If the *parakleetos* (Comforter) is convicting or reproving the world of sin, righteousness, and judgment, certainly there is more to the masculine *parakleetos* than just comfort. I would assume the same of the feminine *paraklesis*. It is very likely that *paraklesis* (exhortation) involves beseeching, admonition, or even reproving (in the fruits of love and humility).

So we have established that the Holy Spirit is the Comforter, or *parakleetos* (John 14:16), who is to call us alongside to convict us of sin and warn us of the evils of this world. In a similar fashion, the manifestation of prophecy by the Spirit is for the saints to call us alongside them as well. The masculine word is used when God the Holy Spirit does it directly, and the feminine word is used when God indirectly calls man alongside Him using His bride, the saints. Either way, the function of the Holy Spirit in prophecy involves call-ing another to the side in a relationship, either directly (*parakleetos*) or through the body of Christ (*paraklesis*).

The implication of consolation in the definition of *paraklesis* presents a beautiful picture. When one of my daughters is running and playing in the house, she sometimes falls and begins to cry. If the injury is trivial, I immediately "call her to my side" and have her sit in my lap. I hold her and console her until the tears are gone. When she is ready, she goes on playing as though nothing ever happened. This is my job as a father. This is the comfort aspect of *paraklesis*. However, *paraklesis* might include comments, such as "You need to be more careful" or "This is why we should not run in the house." *Paraklesis* is consolation but probably includes admo-nition as well.

It is interesting that I see my wife do exactly the same thing. In fact, she is better equipped for comfort than I am. Yet, when she is comforting, it is still an expression of my desire for the family and thus a reflection of me. This is part of the picture of *paraklesis* and *parakleetos*. The Husband, Christ, through the Holy Spirit (*parakleetos*), can console us, just as I do my children. In the same way, the bride (or body) of Christ provides consolation as an expression or reflection of the Husband (*parakleetos*). In fact, the wife should reflect the husband as we reflect Christ. This consola-tion (*paraklesis*) by the bride of Christ occurs by the manifes-tation of prophecy.

It is probably no coincidence that for years I have played this game with my children where I'll tell them I have a secret. When I say this, they run over close to me so I can whisper in their ears. For many years they would run quickly in anticipation of some hidden wisdom or mystery, but the secret was always "I love you." Now they simply look at me and say, "I know, Dad; you love me." Even though they no longer run in expectation of a secret, it is still an encouragement to them every time. Even my teenager, who rolls her eyes at my outdated effort, still deeply wants to know that her daddy loves her. Each time we hear a mystery or secret from the kingdom of God through the manifestation of prophecy, it is as if our Father in heaven is saying, "I love you." I do not play this game with children other than mine, and God does not usually prophesy to children other than His. "Wherefore tongues are for a sign, not to them that believe, but to them that believe not: *but prophesying serveth not for them that believe not, but for them which believe* [children of God]" (1 Cor. 14:22, emphasis added).

This point of prophecy being mainly for the children of God brings up another important issue. Only God's children hear His voice: "My sheep hear my voice" (John 10:27). The only way to know we are of God is to hear His words (John 8:47). When we hear His voice through the Holy Spirit and are consoled or admonished, this is the *parakleetos*. This masculine word refers to hearing God directly. Just as sheep are comforted by hearing the shepherd's voice, as my cattle are comforted by hearing my voice in the field, and as my children are comforted by hearing my voice in the house, the children of God are comforted when they hear the voice of the Comforter (*parakleetos*). This direct communication is only for the children of the kingdom.

In a similar fashion, God may speak to His children (and sometimes others) indirectly or through someone else. This someone else is usually His bride. When God speaks through His bride for the purpose of comfort or admonishment, it is signified by the feminine word *paraklesis* and is called *prophecy*. All prophecy originates with hearing His voice. The *parakleetos* (masculine) speaks to us, His bride, and we can then speak this truth to another, which is prophecy and is signified by the feminine world *paraklesis*.

As an analogy, I can give instruction or truth to my children directly (picturing *parakleetos*), or I can tell my bride, and she can inform our children (picturing *paraklesis*). Either way the message came from me, the father. Many may hear the *paraklesis* (prophecy), but only His sheep hear the *parakleetos* (His voice).

Comfort

Paul said, "He that prophesieth speaketh unto men to edification, and exhortation, and comfort" (1 Cor. 14:3). We have examined edification and exhortation, and now we will examine comfort. The Greek word for "comfort" is *paramuthia*, which is also a feminine noun. In this verse, it is interesting that the Greek words translated as "edification", "exhortation", and "comfort" are all the feminine noun forms of these words. They are all functions of the Holy Spirit through the feminine bride, or body of Christ. It is so amazing to read the writings of Paul and see the clear understanding he had of the feminine nature and wifelike responsibility of the bride of Christ. Edification, exhortation, and comfort are all the feminine nouns because they are God's purpose for His bride and are the result of prophecy.

Paramuthia is also difficult to define. It comes from *para*, which can mean "against" or "contrary to," and *muthos*, meaning "a tale, fable, or myth." Paul and Peter both spoke very strongly against such fables (*muthos*) (1 Tim. 1:4, 4:7, 2 Tim. 4:4; Titus 1:14; 2 Peter 1:16). Combining the two, *paramuthia* has the meaning of "contrary to fables," which would mean truth. Thus, *paramuthia* could involve consoling someone with the truth. Since prophecy is revealing the secrets or truth of God, then *paramuthia* may imply speaking the truth (possibly for comfort) and thus correcting a lie (fable). We should examine this further.

Paramuthia, a feminine noun, occurs only once in the New Testament. The neuter noun *paramuthion* occurs only once as well, in Philippians 2:1: "If there be therefore *any consolation [paraklesis] in Christ, if any comfort [paramuthion] of love*, if any fellowship of the Spirit, if any bowels [compassions] and mercies … " Here the neuter form of *paramuthia* is again associated with *paraklesis*. It is difficult to determine the exact meaning from context with just two uses in the New Testament. Since compassion and mercy are also listed in the verse, and knowing that Paul was so explicit in his use of words, I doubt that "comfort" is an accurate rendering of *paramuthia* in the New Testament.

In Colossians 4:11, Paul spoke of "fellowworkers unto the kingdom of God, which have been a *comfort* unto me" (emphasis added). This word "comfort" is translated from *paregoria*, which is again feminine. This is the only occurrence of this word in the New Testament and is regarded as "spoken comfort." The English word *paregoric* is a derivative and describes a comforting medication. Because of the rare occurrences of *paregoria* and *paramuthia* in the New Testament, it is hard to define these words simply as "comfort". It is hard to accept that Paul used so many different words that are now translated as the same word. Single usage makes context very difficult to determine, and other Greek literature is helpful only if it was written within the same time period as the New Testament letters. Therefore, we should look at derivation.

We know that *paramuthia's* derivation is "contrary to or against fables." Of course, that which is contrary to fables or myths is truth, and truth is the wisdom of God hidden in Christ. If we are stewards of these mysteries or truths, then perhaps we are stewards of *paramuthia*: "Neither give heed to *fables* [*muthos*] and endless genealogies, which minister [lead to] questions [doubt], rather than godly *edifying* which is in faith: so do" (1 Tim. 1:4, emphasis added). Here our translations are clearly in error. The word translated as *edifying* is *oikonomia*, which we saw earlier is stewardship and not edification, and the phrase "godly edifying" is actually "a stewardship of God." The verse would literally read, "Do not lead them to fables or endless genealogies which cause doubt, but offer them a stewardship of God in faith." Paul instructed Timothy not to teach fables that cause doubt but to teach "contrary to these fables" (*paramuthia*) and entrust to them a stewardship (1 Cor. 4:1) producing faith. Timothy was not to teach contrary to the secrets of God, but he was to entrust a stewardship of the "true riches" to new disciples. Just as you would entrust money or resources to a manager whom you were training, Timothy was to give these new stewards knowledge (secrets) of God, which they were to oversee (so then, is it possible that an overseer or bishop is just a steward?).

In his second letter, Paul told Timothy, "And the things that thou hast heard of me among many witnesses, *the same commit thou to faithful men, who shall be able to teach others also*" (2:2, emphasis added). As we teach the secrets or truths of God to others, we are entrusting a stewardship to them. We must share these treasures only with "faithful men." We must teach truth (revealed by His Spirit) to correct the lies, fables, and traditions of men. This may be the purpose of prophecy contained in the meaning of *paramuthia*—not comfort.

Refute the False Teaching and Traditions of Men

Over time, false teaching will enter into every church because of our cursed understanding. Consider Paul's last words to the Ephesian elders:

> For I know this, that after my departing shall grievous wolves enter in among you, not sparing the flock. Also of your own selves shall men arise, speaking perverse things, to draw away disciples after them. Therefore watch, and remember, that by the space of three years I ceased not to warn every one night and day with tears. And now, brethren, I commend you to God, and to the word of his grace, which is able to build you up, and to give you an inheritance among all them which are sanctified. (Acts 20:29–32)

For three years, Paul had warned them that wolves (who look like sheep) would arise and live off the flock. Even more, some of the elders (Acts 20:17) he was addressing would teach these "fables," lies, or "perverse things" and draw followers from the body after them (v. 30). To protect against this, Paul attempted to "build [them] up" with prophecy and "give [them] an inheritance" (v. 32). This inheritance was produced through prophecy, and it was a stewardship entrusted to them by Paul to build others in faith. *Paramuthia* would be correcting or refuting the false teaching and traditions (practices) taught by the "wolves."

Pride and impatience can cause us to seek answers within our own understanding and not from the Spirit. These wolves will always have logical, clever answers. When we accept these false teachings, we may begin to build "temples" of doctrine and traditions that cause division among us and do not reflect God's desire for His children to dwell in love and unity. We must be careful not to stray from His "still small voice" (1 Kings 19:12). It is this manifestation or spirit of prophecy that speaks "contrary to or against those fables" (*paramuthia*) to bring the "true" body back to the truth. This is *paramuthia*. Revealing the secret truths or mysteries of God exposes the lies, just as light shines in the darkness. These fables and traditions are the veils or coverings that prophecy removes as the truth is revealed. It is the prophet who, by the Holy Spirit and not by his own understanding, provides correction to the body so that they can be built up in faith (edified).

As we contrast *paramuthia* with *oikodome* (edification), let us look at the picture intended. Prophecy builds on the foundation (Jesus Christ) using the treasures of gold, silver, and precious stones to increase the faith of the individual. As time passes, inferior building materials—wood, hay, and stubble—are inserted by "grievous wolves" (Acts 20:29–30) under the direction of an enemy (Satan). These inferior materials weaken the building (causing doubt), and it no longer can withstand the storms, and it begins to lean. The true riches—gold, silver, and precious stones—strengthen our building (edification) by increasing our faith. It is the prophet who corrects or refutes the fables (wood, hay, and stubble) that lead to doubt. Prophets, under the influence of the Holy Spirit, stand "against the fables" (*paramuthia*), thus exposing the inferior materials so that the building up (edification) can continue.

Can we prevent these inferior building products from being included? Yes, we must continually sacrifice our understanding and be taught by the Spirit of prophecy, who is the witness of Jesus (Rev. 19:10). Furthermore, any revelation we receive must be tested against the Scriptures over time. We must search from Genesis to Revelation. This is the refining fire (Rev. 3:18), and this is how we test the qualities of our building materials as we seek to edify (build up).

Paul said, "For if we would judge ourselves, we should not be judged" (1 Cor. 11:31). If we would judge our understanding ourselves by testing it against Scripture, we would not be judged and blinded like the Pharisees (John 9:39–41). Judgment is the refining fire of the Lord (1 Cor. 3:13–15). As we test our understanding against the Scripture (refining fire) like the Bereans, the wood, hay, and stubble (lies and fables) will burn, thus purifying the gold, silver, and precious stones (truth or secrets of God). By testing all revelations we receive in the refining fire, we protect against fables (Rev. 3:1–16). As we teach "against or contrary to fables" (*paramuthia*), we are edifying or building up the body.

We have seen that the manifestation of prophecy is Spirit-led and reveals the hidden truths or secrets of the kingdom of God for the benefit of the body of Christ. Where tongues can edify only the one speaking, prophecy edifies or builds the body of Christ in faith, each on his own foundation, which is Jesus. First Corinthians 14:3 says that not only does prophecy edify or build up the body, but it exhorts (probably with warning) and corrects (with the truth) by exposing the fables or lies. As we are given these true riches or knowledge of Him, we are given a stewardship. As we teach or reveal truth to others, we are entrusting them with a stewardship for the purpose of building up, comforting, warning, and correcting lies.

Chapter 10
A More Excellent Way

Before we conclude, we should return to the beginning. We started with 1 Corinthians 13:1, but Paul wrote this letter without chapter or verse divisions. Chapter divisions were added in the thirteenth century, and verses were added in the sixteenth century. The last verse of 1 Corinthians 12 actually sets up chapter 13: "But covet earnestly the best gifts: and yet shew I unto you *a more excellent way*" (v. 31, emphasis added). All of chapter 13 speaks of the superiority of the fruit of love over the spiritual gifts, and love is the "more excellent way": "Though I speak with the tongues of men and of angels ... And though I have the gift of prophecy, and understand all mysteries, and all knowledge ... *and have not charity* [love], *I am nothing*" (vv. 1–2, emphasis added). Love is greater than knowledge, prophecy, and, obviously, tongues.

Fruit is more important than knowledge. Earlier, we looked at Ephesians 3:19: "And to know the love of Christ,

106

which passeth knowledge …," Literally, Paul was explaining that love surpasses knowledge. The Greek word for "passeth" is *huperballo,* meaning "to excel or surpass." The love of Christ (love that comes from Christ) excels or surpasses knowledge. You can have knowledge without love, and we should not look for knowledge without fruit. Jesus never said you would know them by their knowledge: "Wherefore by their *fruits* [such as love] ye shall know them" (Matt. 7:20, emphasis added). The evidence of God's Spirit in a person is the fruit of the Spirit, not necessarily knowledge, prophecy, or tongues.

In the same way, fruit is better than prophecy:

> Wherefore by their fruits ye shall know them.
> Not every one that saith unto me, Lord, Lord,
> shall enter into the kingdom of heaven; but he
> that doeth the will of my Father, which is in
> heaven. *Many will say to me in that day, Lord,
> Lord, have we not prophesied in thy name?* and in
> thy name have cast out devils? and in thy name
> done many wonderful works? And then will I
> profess unto them, I never knew you: depart
> from me, ye that work iniquity. (Matt. 7:20–23,
> emphasis added)

There will be those who prophesied yet never knew (*ginosko*) Christ. They never were intimate with Him and did not yield fruit. Fruit is greater than prophecy. The first commandment (Gen. 1:28) is to bear fruit, not to prophesy.

The fruit of the Spirit is better than the gold of this world, as well as the "gold" in the kingdom of God: "*My fruit is better than gold*, yea, than fine gold; and *my revenue than choice silver*" (Prov. 8:19, emphasis added). This "fine gold" is pure from the Refiner's fire and represents pure knowledge or prophecy, not the partial or incomplete we have today. Fruit is also better "than choice silver." The Hebrew word for "revenue" is *tebuwah* and means "fruit or increase." The revenue or increase each year is fruit. God also refers to "the fruit of thy body [children], and the fruit of thy ground [crops], and the fruit of thy cattle [calves]" (Deut. 28:4), all speaking of fruit (or increase) that comes from the Lord. Paul said that we can plant and water, "but God ... giveth the increase" (1 Cor. 3:7). This increase in fruit is better than "fine gold" and "choice silver," better than knowledge or prophecy. This valued "fruit of the Spirit is love, joy, peace, longsuffering, gentleness, goodness, faith, meekness, temperance: against such there is no law" (Gal. 5:22–23).

In the Scriptures, knowledge and revelation are the "true riches" and pictured as gold, silver, and precious stones. These are wonderful things, yet they do not give or sustain life. It is the fruit that sustains or gives life. The "flesh" of the fruit is food, and the seeds give life. When famine or destruction comes, people will throw their gold and silver in the streets (Ezek. 7:19) because they cannot eat it. When judgment comes, it is not our knowledge that God seeks; He desires our fruit. The harvest is always for fruit, and the spiritual harvest at the end of the age is for spiritual fruit, not for souls or knowledge.

Even the design of heaven reveals the superiority of fruit over knowledge of Him. The gold and precious jewels that represent the knowledge of His secrets make up the walls, gates, and streets of heaven. They are peripheral and on the outside. However, the fruit of the Spirit on the tree of life lies at the very center of heaven, even "in the midst of the street of it [God's throne], and on either side of the river [of water of life]" (Rev. 22:2). It is the twelve fruits of the tree of life that are of great value to God. Again, fruit is more important than knowledge: "Wherefore by their fruits ye will know them" (Matt. 7:20).

The Seed Is in the Fruit

Prophecy and knowledge will not multiply the kingdom of God, only fruit will. Prophecy may edify or encourage growth in an individual Christian but not increase the kingdom in numbers. The spiritual seed, which multiplies the spiritual kingdom of God, is found only within the fruit of the Spirit. Just as an apple contains apple seed inside, God's seed is inside His fruit. People do not receive the Lord Jesus from our message (teachings and prophecy); they receive Jesus from our fruit. People may join our fellowship or support our ministry because of our message, but they can enter God's spiritual kingdom only by the spiritual seed inside the fruit of the Spirit that we manifest.

"Be fruitful and multiply" is the first commandment recorded in the Bible (Gen. 1:28), given to Adam. Later, it was given to Noah (Gen. 9:1), Abraham (Gen. 17:2–6), Jacob (Gen. 35:11), as well as to Jacob's children through Moses (Lev. 26:9). In fact, much of Jesus' teachings concerned fruit, for if we do not bear fruit, we will not have any seed, and we cannot multiply His kingdom. We will recognize "true" Christians by their fruit, not by their message. If we were less "message"-oriented and more fruit-oriented, we would have more unity in the body of Christ today.

When we speak of one who is mature, we should speak of fruit, not of knowledge. It is fruit, that when mature, has seeds, not knowledge. Only ripe or mature fruit will have mature seeds that can reproduce. Whether it is an apple, a grape, a heifer, or a young person, there must be a certain amount of physical maturity before it can reproduce. In the same way, we must have mature love, joy, peace, longsuffering, gentleness, goodness, faith, meekness, and temperance to have ripe seed to reproduce the kingdom of God.

Some come to God but seek only knowledge and wisdom. Because they lack the fruit of patience, they receive the teachings and traditions of men instead. Yes, there is truth mixed into all these teachings. Satan usually mixes his lies in truth like leaven in the meal (Matt. 13:33). Many unknowingly teach lies just as confidently as truth. As we receive revelation, we must be humble (fruit) and patient (fruit) in searching the Scriptures like the Bereans. The fruit of humility, patience, gentleness, goodness, mercy, faith, and love must be present and somewhat mature before "we speak the wisdom of God in a mystery, even the hidden wisdom, which God ordained before the world unto our glory" (1 Cor. 2:7).

Examine Your Heart

Fruit does not come from biblical knowledge but from the condition of our hearts. In the parable of the sower (Matt. 13; Mark 4; Luke 8), the soils represent the hearts of men. Only the "good soil," representing a good heart, produced fruit. Just as my family must prepare the soil on our farm each year to yield a fruitful harvest, we must prepare our hearts to produce the fruit of the Spirit.

In addition, prophecy and knowledge, the "true riches" of God, come not from biblical knowledge but from the condition of the heart as well. In Luke 16, where we began our study of the "true riches," Jesus said,

> No servant can serve two masters: for either he
> will hate the one, and love the other; or else he
> will hold to the one, and despise the other. Ye
> cannot serve God and mammon. And the
> Pharisees also, who were covetous, heard all these

things: and they derided him. *And he said unto them, Ye are they which justify yourselves before men; but God knoweth your hearts: for that which is highly esteemed among men is abomination in the sight of God.* (Luke 16:13–15, emphasis added)

The Pharisees knew the Scriptures better than any group in history, and yet because of their hearts, they crucified the Lord of glory. Jesus acknowledged their knowledge of Scripture yet condemned their evil hearts that trusted in man instead of the Father:

Search the scriptures; for in them ye think ye have eternal life: and they are they which testify of me. And ye will not come to me, that ye might have life. I receive not honour from men. But I know you, that ye have not the love of God in you. I am come in my Father's name, and ye receive me not: if another shall come in his own name, him ye will receive. How can ye believe, which receive honour one of another, and seek not the honour that cometh from God only? Do not think that I will accuse you to the Father: *there is one that accuseth you, even Moses in whom ye trust. For had ye believed Moses, ye would have believed me: for he wrote of me. But if ye believe not his writings, how shall ye believe my words?* (John 5:39–47, emphasis added)

Even though the Pharisees knew the Scriptures inside and out, they did not know Jesus. They claimed to trust in Moses and they claimed his name. They told Jesus that they were "Moses' disciples" (John 9:28), but they obviously did not really trust in what Moses wrote, or they would have known the Messiah who was standing in front of them. These Pharisees were deceived in their hearts. Thinking they were seeking God, they were merely seeking to build their own kingdom and look good before the people. They were covetous of money, as well as power, and did not seek to please God. In their hearts, they merely desired to look good (spiritual) and knowledgeable before men. They had no revelation or insight from the Spirit, but merely taught their own understanding or that of their sects.

Worse yet, they clouded the lines between what Scripture said and how they interpreted it, making law out of their traditions. Jesus spoke to them, quoting Isaiah, saying, "And he said unto them, Full well ye reject the commandment of God, that ye may keep your own traditions"; and "But in vain they do worship me, *teaching for doctrines the commandments of men*" (Mark 7:9; Matt. 15:9, emphasis added). This hypocrisy is an abomination in the sight of God.

Today may not be much different. We have modern-day Pharisees interpreting the Scriptures unto themselves instead of receiving revelation from the Spirit. They take their own traditions and teachings, which may not be of the Scriptures, and teach strongly that they are. They may say they are the disciples of Jesus, just as the Pharisees claimed to be disciples of Moses, but are they? Jesus said of them, "For many shall come in my name, saying, I [Jesus] am Christ; and shall deceive many" (Matt. 24:5). These modern Pharisees come in the name of Jesus *and say that Jesus is the Messiah*, the anointed Christ of God, but they deceive many by their outward behavior. Just like the Pharisees of Jesus' day, they are deceived and believe they are seeking God as they try to justify themselves before men to keep their power and their positions. God knows their hearts, and we will not be deceived either, if we just look for fruit.

We must be careful not to judge these Pharisees too harshly, for we all have these tendencies. It is the curse from Adam. We must be humble and allow the Spirit of God to search our hearts and reveal our hypocrisy, for His power is made perfect in our weakness (humility) (2 Cor. 12:9–10). We should never fear what man thinks but merely seek to have right and humble hearts toward God. A heart designed to love God and serve others by abounding in the fruit of His Spirit is what God desires.

If our hearts are right with God, He will not condemn our actions. However, man will condemn us. The same people who loved us for our hypocrisy and "religious" behavior will hate us for our manifestations of His Spirit, in particular for the fruit of the Spirit. Those who liked us with our pride and selfishness will now hate us for our fruit of humility and love. Those who loved you for following men's tradition will now hate you for your revelation by God's Spirit. Yet, God gives revelation of Himself only to a "right" heart: "Blessed are the pure in heart: for they shall see God" (Matt. 5:8).

Concluding Thoughts

As we humble ourselves and draw closer to God, He will open our eyes and ears so that we may see and hear His mysteries, for "he revealeth his secret unto his servants the prophets" (Amos 3:7). These hidden truths are the "true riches" of the kingdom of God, and as we prove ourselves faithful as lowly servants, we may become stewards of these "riches." For now, we will receive only part of these riches, but when the "perfect" appears, the partial will dissolve in the glory of His coming, and we will know fully of His splendor.

In the meantime, He has given us prophecy to build up, comfort, warn, and correct the many lies of the enemy, but we must be careful how we build. We must build from the revelation of His Spirit as we excavate the bottomless mine shaft called the knowledge of God. The walls of the mine scintillate with gold, silver, and precious stones, which represent the knowledge of God. This intimate knowledge of God is hidden in the form of mysteries and revealed by prophecy.

BIBLIOGRAPHY

Work Cited

Holy Bible. King James Version. 1769 Cambridge edition.

Concordances:

Strong, James. The New Strong's Exhaustive Concordance of the Bible. Nashville, TN: Thomas Nelson, 1996.

Wigram, George V., ed. The Englishman's Hebrew Concordance of the New Testament. Peabody, MA: Hendrickson, 1999.

———. The Englishman's Hebrew Concordance of the Old Testament. Peabody, MA: Hendrickson, 1999.

Interlinears:

Marshall, Alfred, trans. Parallel New Testament in Greek and English. Grand Rapids, MI: Zondervan, 1980.

Green, Jay P., trans. The Interlinear Greek-English New Testament. Grand Rapids, MI: Baker, 1996.

———. The Interlinear Hebrew-English Old Testament. Lafayette, IN: Sovereign Grace, 2000.

Lexicons:

Brown, Francis, S. Driver, and Charles Briggs. The Brown-Driver-Briggs Hebrew and English Lexicon. Peabody, MA: Hendrickson, 1999.

Vine, W.E. Vine's Complete Expository Dictionary of Old and New Testament Words. Nashville, TN: Thomas Nelson, 1996.

Zodhiates, Spiros, ed. The Complete Word Study Dictionary New Testament. Chattanooga, TN: AMG International, 1993.